Easy to Use

PICK UP & PLAY

HOW TO READ
MUSIC
ESSENTIAL SKILLS

SEE IT ■ HEAR IT

JAKE JACKSON

mobile
online

Flame Tree
Music
BOOKS • eBOOKS • RESOURCES

C334017139

Contents

Publisher/Creative Director: Nick Wells • **Layout Design:** Jane Ashley • **Website and Software:** David Neville with Stevens Dumpala and Steve Moulton • **Editorial:** Gillian Whitaker

First published 2016 by
FLAME TREE PUBLISHING
6 Melbray Mews, Fulham,
London SW6 3NS, United Kingdom
flametreepublishing.com

Music information site: flametreemusic.com

16 17 18 19 20 21 22 • 1 2 3 4 5 6 7 8 9 10

© 2016 Flame Tree Publishing Ltd

All images and notation courtesy of Flame Tree Publishing Ltd, except the following: keyboard and guitar diagrams © 2016 Jake Jackson/Flame Tree Publishing Ltd. Courtesy of Shutterstock.com and copyright the following photographers: Stokkete 8, 31, 65; paolo jacopo medda 13; Tomas Smolek 14; Shykor Oleksandr 19; Ariel Schrotter 22, 104; Mehmet Dilsiz 31; bango 34; Mark Yuill 49; Pavel L Photo and Video 51; SP-Photo 58; Vadym Zaitsev 60; LIUSHENGFILM 62; Ana Martinez de Mingo 72; Remus Moise 74; otnaydur 85; Mutita Narkmuang 158; Claudio Divizia 172; Africa Studio175.

Every effort has been made to contact copyright holders. We apologize in advance for any omissions and would be pleased to insert the appropriate acknowledgement in subsequent editions of this publication.

Android is a trademark of Google Inc. Logic Pro, iPhone and iPad are either registered trademarks or trademarks of Apple Computer Inc. in the United States and/or other countries. Cubase is a registered trademark or trademark of Steinberg Media Technologies GmbH, a wholly owned subsidiary of Yamaha Corporation, in the United States and/or other countries. Nokia's product names are either trademarks or registered trademarks of Nokia. Nokia is a registered trademark of Nokia Corporation in the United States and/or other countries. Samsung and Galaxy S are both registered trademarks of Samsung Electronics America, Ltd. in the United States and/or other countries.

This book is an adaptation of *Reading Music Made Easy* by Jake Jackson, originally published in 2013.

Jake Jackson (author) is a writer and musician. He has created and contributed to over 25 practical music books, including *Reading Music Made Easy*. His music is available on iTunes, Amazon and Spotify amongst others.

Printed in China

Reading Music
An Introduction

This book is divided into seven sections. If you follow these, and keep referring back to the tips and diagrams, you will soon be able to recognize, understand and even produce your own musical notation.

1. **All the Basics** introduces the core features of music on the page, including the stave, clefs and notes.

2. **Notes & Timing** outlines the duration of different notes and their corresponding rests. It also looks at Time Signatures and their role in establishing rhythm.

3. **Pitch** provides tips on learning the notes of the Treble and Bass Clefs, as well as showing how they would be played on the piano and guitar. This section also covers sharp and flat notes.

4. **Keys** are determined by the combination of sharps or flats. Learning to identify key signatures in notation can help you see and predict how a piece of music will develop.

5. **Scales** are extremely useful in understanding the relationship between notes in a piece of music, in any given key.

6. **Common Chords** gives many of the chords that you are likely to come across in major keys.

7. **Extra Notation** covers expressional marks, which are additional stylistic instructions related to speed, dynamics and articulation. Musical terms indicate how a piece should be played, and therefore how it will sound.

START
HERE

ALL THE
BASICS

NOTES &
TIMING

PITCH

KEYS

SCALES

COMMON
CHORDS

EXTRA
NOTATION

The Diagrams
A Quick Guide

In this book, where notes are given, their positions and notation for both the piano and the guitar are also shown to help you visualize how the notes translate to these instruments.

The piano diagrams are pretty straightforward, but the guitar ones may need further explanation.

Guitar Tabs

All the diagrams are shown from the player's view, as if you were looking down at the guitar while holding it. The Low E – the thickest string, also known as the 6th string – is closest to the player's eyes, and shown at the bottom of these diagrams. The High E – the thinnest string, also known as the 1st string – is closer to the floor, and shown at the top of these diagrams. Some diagrams show a bass guitar, which typically has four strings instead of five.

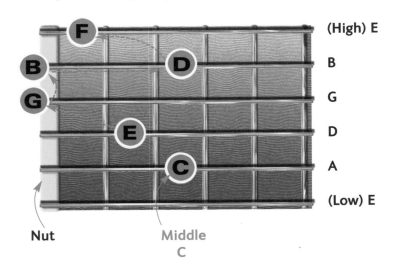

Nut   Middle
       C

Scan to **HEAR** the C major chord, and access the full library of scales and chords on flametreemusic.com

TAB notation

Some guitarists use tablature (called TAB) instead of staves. The six lines represent the six strings of the guitar, from the high E string to the low E string, and the numbers represent the frets that produce the notes. A zero indicates that the string is played open. In the below example, the first C is played on the 5th string – the A string – by holding down the third fret along.

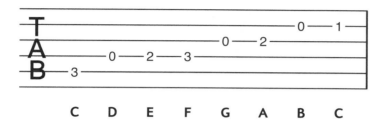

C   D   E   F   G   A   B   C

A Note About Middle C

A knowledge of middle C is useful in understanding music written for different instruments, the relationship between the treble and bass clefs and pitch generally. Further information on middle C can be found on page 21.

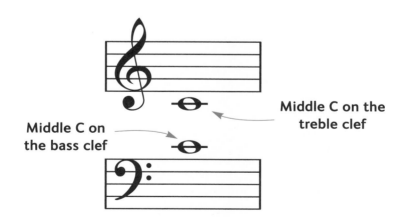

Middle C on the treble clef

Middle C on the bass clef

START
HERE

ALL THE
BASICS

NOTES &
TIMING

PITCH

KEYS

SCALES

COMMON
CHORDS

EXTRA
NOTATION

The Sound Links
Another Quick Guide

Requirements: a camera and internet-ready smartphone (e.g. **iPhone**, any **Android** phone (e.g. **Samsung Galaxy**), **Nokia Lumia**, or **camera-enabled tablet** such as the **iPad Mini**). The best result is achieved using a WIFI connection.

1. Download any **free QR code reader**. An app store search will reveal a great many of these, so obviously it's best to go with the ones with the highest ratings and don't be afraid to try a few before you settle on the one that works best for you. Tapmedia's QR Reader app is good, or ATT Scanner (used below) or QR Media. Some of the free apps have ads, which can be annoying.

2. On your smartphone, open the app and **scan** the **QR code** at the base of any particular page.

FREE ACCESS on iPhone & Android etc, using any free QR code app

Scan to **HEAR** the C major chord, and access the full library of scales and chords on flametreemusic.com

7

3. For the scales and chord sections, each code at the bottom of the page will bring you to the relevant scale or chord on flametreemusic.com. Scanning the code on all other pages will bring you to the C major chord, and from there you can access and hear the complete library of scales and chords.

FREE ACCESS on iPhone & Android etc, using any free QR code app

Scan to **HEAR** the C major chord, and access the full library of scales and chords on flametreemusic.com

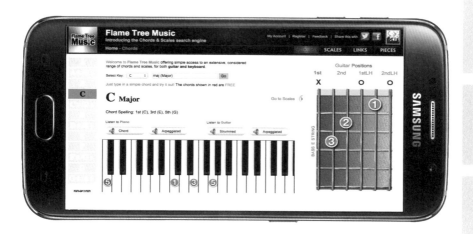

4. Use the drop down menu to choose from **20 scales** or 12 **free chords** (50 with subscription) per key.

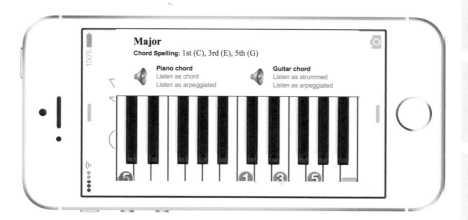

5. Click the sounds! Both piano and guitar audio is provided. This is particularly helpful when you're playing with others.

The QR codes give you direct access to chords and scales. You can access a much wider range of chords if you register and subscribe.

FREE ACCESS on iPhone & Android etc, using any free QR code app

Scan to **HEAR** the C major chord, and access the full library of scales and chords on flametreemusic.com

START
HERE

ALL THE
BASICS

NOTES &
TIMING

PITCH

KEYS

SCALES

COMMON
CHORDS

EXTRA
NOTATION

Music on the Page

START HERE

ALL THE BASICS

NOTES & TIMING

PITCH

KEYS

SCALES

COMMON CHORDS

EXTRA NOTATION

Music is created by people singing and playing a wide variety of instruments. Writing down and reading the music is an important part of **music-making**.

The following pages will introduce you to the very basic concepts: what is a **stave**? What are **lines** and **spaces**? What are **ledger lines** and **clefs**?

This section closes with the note called **middle C**, the understanding of which will give you a solid foundation for the rest of the book.

FREE ACCESS on iPhone & Android etc, using any free QR code app

Scan to **HEAR** the C major chord, and access the full library of scales and chords on flametreemusic.com

Stave or Staff

These five lines make up the stave (which is sometimes called the staff).

The stave is the backbone to the body of the music. It holds the **notes** and the **rests** and the various **symbols** that tell you how to play loudly or softly, when to repeat and when to stop.

The stave allows us to indicate **pitch**: whether a sound is high or low.

The highest sounds appear at the top of a stave.

The lowest sounds appear at the bottom of a stave.

Scan to **HEAR** the C major chord, and access the full library of scales and chords on flametreemusic.com

START
HERE

ALL THE
BASICS

NOTES &
TIMING

PITCH

KEYS

SCALES

COMMON
CHORDS

EXTRA
NOTATION

Lines

The stave is always made up of five lines. Notes can be written on the lines or in the spaces.

Each line on a stave represents a particular musical note, although which note depends on which **clef** is shown at the beginning of the music (clefs are introduced on pages 16–19, and covered in detail on pages 50–79).

It is worth noting that the lines also show the music **moving** in time from **start** to **finish**, and should always be read from **left** to **right**.

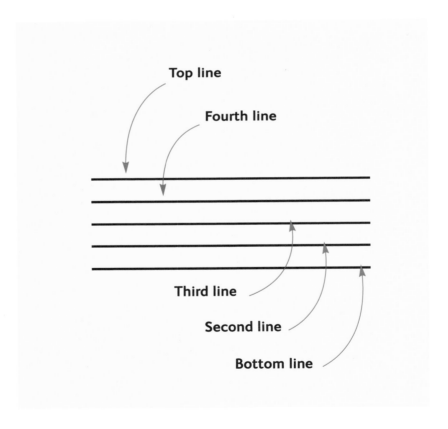

FREE ACCESS on iPhone & Android etc, using any free QR code app

Scan to **HEAR** the C major chord, and access the full library of scales and chords on flametreemusic.com

Spaces

Between the five lines there are four spaces. Notes can also be placed in these spaces.

The **higher** the **space** in the stave, the **higher** the **note**.

There are spaces **above** and **below** the stave. These can also hold notes.

ALL THE
BASICS

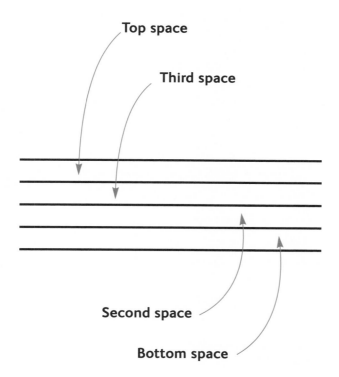

Top space

Third space

Second space

Bottom space

FREE ACCESS on iPhone & Android etc, using any free QR code app

Scan to **HEAR** the C major chord, and access the full library of scales and chords on flametreemusic.com

Ledger Lines

Often you will see music with small lines written above or below the main part of the stave.

These are called **ledger lines**.

Ledger lines are only used when a note is written in a **space** or on a **line** where the note is higher or lower than those on the main part of the stave.

Ledger lines are written at equal distances from the main lines.

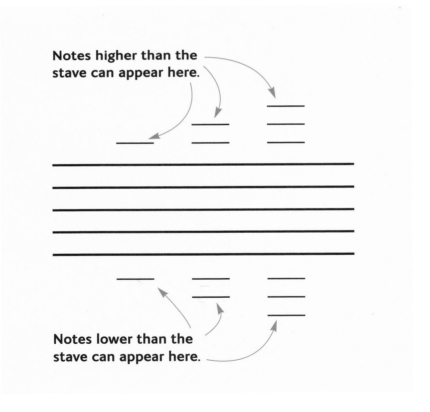

Notes higher than the stave can appear here.

Notes lower than the stave can appear here.

Scan to **HEAR** the C major chord, and access the full library of scales and chords on flametreemusic.com

START HERE

ALL THE BASICS

NOTES & TIMING

PITCH

KEYS

SCALES

COMMON CHORDS

EXTRA NOTATION

START
HERE

ALL THE
BASICS

NOTES &
TIMING

PITCH

KEYS

SCALES

COMMON
CHORDS

EXTRA
NOTATION

FREE ACCESS on iPhone & Android etc, using any free QR code app

Scan to **HEAR** the C major chord, and access the full library of scales and chords on flametreemusic.com

START
HERE

**ALL THE
BASICS**

NOTES &
TIMING

PITCH

KEYS

SCALES

COMMON
CHORDS

EXTRA
NOTATION

FREE ACCESS on iPhone & Android
etc, using any free QR code app

Scan to **HEAR** the C major chord, and
access the full library of scales and
chords on flametreemusic.com

The Bars

When you look at music you will normally see a series of vertical lines placed at intervals along the stave.

These are called **bar lines**. The area between each bar line is called a **bar**. Sometimes these are called **measures**.

Written music, called **notation**, is grouped into bars to provide structure to the notes, to make it easier to follow, and to show the **beat** of the music.

The **first bar** on each stave on a page of music always carries a **clef** symbol in place of the first bar line.

START
HERE

ALL THE
BASICS

NOTES &
TIMING

PITCH

KEYS

SCALES

COMMON
CHORDS

EXTRA
NOTATION

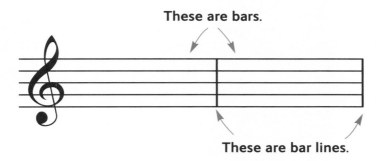

These are bars.

These are bar lines.

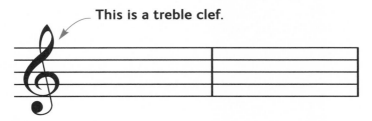

This is a treble clef.

FREE ACCESS on iPhone & Android etc, using any free QR code app

Scan to **HEAR** the C major chord, and access the full library of scales and chords on flametreemusic.com

START
HERE

ALL THE
BASICS

NOTES &
TIMING

PITCH

KEYS

SCALES

COMMON
CHORDS

EXTRA
NOTATION

Introducing Clefs

A clef symbol is written at the beginning of a piece of music, and at the beginning, on the left side, of every stave. Clefs signify the range of pitches that are in use.

The Treble Clef

The **treble clef** is used for instruments that sound higher, usually above **middle C** (see page 21 for information on middle C). It is also known the 'G' clef, as the note 'G' is signified by the line that the curl wraps around.

The curl of the treble clef wraps around the second line up from the bottom line.

Numbered from the bottom line upwards

FREE ACCESS on iPhone & Android etc, using any free QR code app

Scan to **HEAR** the C major chord, and access the full library of scales and chords on flametreemusic.com

The Bass Clef

The **bass clef** is used for instruments and voices that sound lower, especially those that provide the bass sounds in a piece of music.

It is sometimes referred to as the 'F' clef, as the note 'F' is indicated by where the clef sits on the stave.

The two dots of the bass clef sit either side of fourth line up from the bottom line.

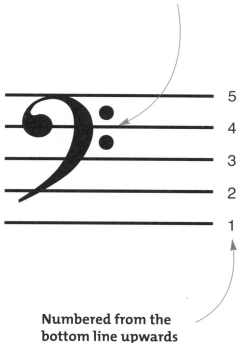

Numbered from the bottom line upwards

The C Clef

Other clefs are occasionally used for different instruments to make the reading of the music easier for them. These include the alto clef and the tenor clef (also called C clefs).

The **alto clef** can be used by the **viola**. The middle of this clef sits on the line that normally holds middle C.

The middle of the alto clef sits on the line that normally shows middle C.

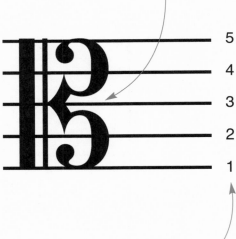

5
4
3
2
1

Numbered from the bottom line upwards

FREE ACCESS on iPhone & Android etc, using any free QR code app

Scan to **HEAR** the C major chord, and access the full library of scales and chords on flametreemusic.com

The C clef is useful for instruments whose range is **neither entirely above or below middle C**. This clef allows their usual range of notes to be recorded on the main stave, without too many **ledger lines**. The centre of the C clef indicates the location of **middle C**, and it can be positioned elsewhere on the stave, as in the diagram below.

The **tenor clef** sits on the **fourth** line of the stave, allowing the stave to cover a range slightly **lower** than the alto clef (but still higher than the bass clef). The tenor clef can be used by the **cello**, **bassoon** and **trombone**.

START HERE

ALL THE BASICS

NOTES & TIMING

PITCH

KEYS

SCALES

COMMON CHORDS

EXTRA NOTATION

The middle of the tenor clef sits on the line that normally shows middle C.

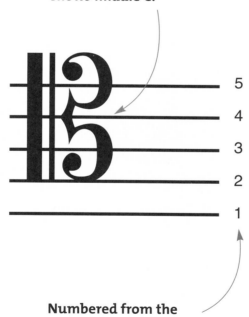

Numbered from the bottom line upwards

Scan to **HEAR** the C major chord, and access the full library of scales and chords on flametreemusic.com

Parts of a Note

START
HERE

ALL THE BASICS

Notes are made up of:

1. A **notehead** that is either hollow or filled.

2. A **stem**, if the note is shorter in length.

3. A **tail**, if the note is even shorter in length. The shorter the length, the more tails it has. When connecting notes of the same value, this becomes a **Beam**. A semiquaver has two tails, so connects to other semiquavers using two beams.

NOTES &
TIMING

PITCH

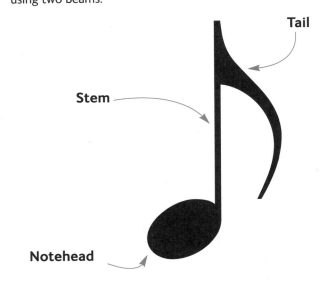

Tail

Stem

Notehead

KEYS

SCALES

Beam

This is a crotchet rest (see page 37).

COMMON
CHORDS

Notes below the third line are written with their stems up. For beamed notes, the note furthest from the third line determines the stem direction.

EXTRA
NOTATION

FREE ACCESS on iPhone & Android etc, using any free QR code app

Scan to **HEAR** the C major chord, and access the full library of scales and chords on flametreemusic.com

Middle C

One of the most useful notes to know about is middle C.

It is usually the **lowest note** that an instrument using a **treble clef** can play. It is located in the middle of the piano keyboard.

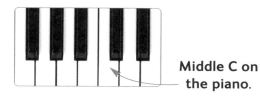

Middle C on the piano.

In notation, middle C appears on the first ledger line **below** the **treble clef** and the first ledger line **above** the **bass clef**. Middle C sits exactly between the treble and bass clef staves.

To make the reading and writing of notation easier, the gap between the staves of the treble and bass clef is usually stretched out to allow a middle C on **both** staves.

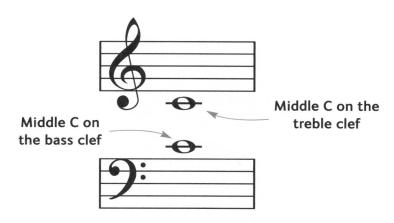

Middle C on the treble clef

Middle C on the bass clef

FREE ACCESS on iPhone & Android etc, using any free QR code app

Scan to **HEAR** the C major chord, and access the full library of scales and chords on flametreemusic.com

Note Values

START HERE

ALL THE BASICS

NOTES & TIMING

PITCH

KEYS

SCALES

COMMON CHORDS

EXTRA NOTATION

Notes are the main building blocks of every musical piece.

The **position** of the note on a particular stave tells you which note to play.

The **look of the note** tells you how long to sound the note and therefore gives you clues about the pulse of the music and how it relates to the time signature (see pages 40–49).

Notes can be **grouped** together and must be replaced by an equivalent rest (see pages 34–39) if no sound is to be played.

Scan to **HEAR** the C major chord, and access the full library of scales and chords on flametreemusic.com

Note Relationships

This table of **note values** shows how different lengths of notes relate to each other. As you can see, one semibreve is equal to two minims, which is equal to four crotchets, and so on. A standard musical bar lasts for **a whole note**, or four quarter notes. We will look at the individual types of notes in more detail on the following pages, where the bar examples assume this standard length.

Whole note	① Semibreve
Half notes	② Minims
Quarter notes	③ Crotchets
Eighth notes	④ Quavers
Sixteenth notes	⑤ Semiquavers

FREE ACCESS on iPhone & Android etc, using any free QR code app

Scan to **HEAR** the C major chord, and access the full library of scales and chords on flametreemusic.com

Whole Note/Semibreve

A semibreve is a note that fills a standard whole bar, hence the alternative name: whole note.

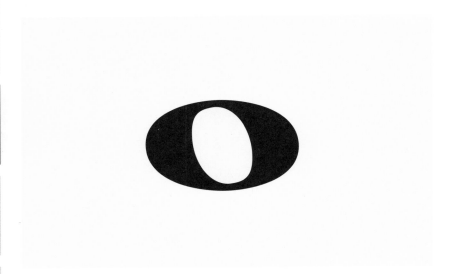

A semibreve has a **hollow notehead**, with no stem.

A semibreve is equal to two minims, four crotchets or eight quavers.

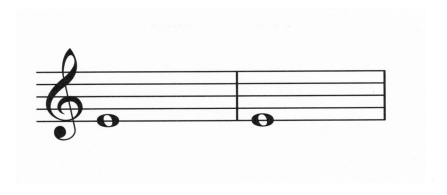

FREE ACCESS on iPhone & Android etc, using any free QR code app

Scan to **HEAR** the C major chord, and access the full library of scales and chords on flametreemusic.com

Sidebar navigation:

START HERE

ALL THE BASICS

NOTES & TIMING

PITCH

KEYS

SCALES

COMMON CHORDS

EXTRA NOTATION

Half Note/Minim

A minim is a note that fills half of a standard whole bar, hence the alternative name: half note.

A minim has a **hollow notehead** and a stem, but no tail.

A minim is equal to two crotchets, four quavers or eight semiquavers.

Scan to **HEAR** the C major chord, and access the full library of scales and chords on flametreemusic.com

NOTES & TIMING

Quarter Note/Crotchet

A crochet is a note that makes up a quarter of a standard whole bar, hence the alternative name: quarter note.

A crotchet has a **filled-in notehead** and a stem, but no tail.

A crotchet is equal to half a minim, two quavers or four semiquavers.

FREE ACCESS on iPhone & Android etc, using any free QR code app

Scan to **HEAR** the C major chord, and access the full library of scales and chords on flametreemusic.com

START HERE

ALL THE BASICS

NOTES & TIMING

PITCH

KEYS

SCALES

COMMON CHORDS

EXTRA NOTATION

2. NOTES & TIMING

Eighth Note/Quaver

A quaver is a note that makes up an eighth of a standard whole bar, hence the alternative name: eighth note.

A quaver has a filled-in notehead, a stem, **a tail** and beams.

A quaver is equal to two semiquavers.

A single quaver is written with its tail, but quavers are more commonly found in groups with a beam across, to make them easier to read.

This is a quaver rest (see page 38).

FREE ACCESS on iPhone & Android etc, using any free QR code app

Scan to **HEAR** the C major chord, and access the full library of scales and chords on flametreemusic.com

START HERE

ALL THE BASICS

NOTES & TIMING

PITCH

KEYS

SCALES

COMMON CHORDS

EXTRA NOTATION

Sixteenth Note/Semiquaver

A semiquaver is a note that makes up a sixteenth of a standard whole bar, hence the alternative name: sixteenth note.

A semiquaver has a filled-in notehead, a stem and **two tails**, which become **double beams** when grouped with other semiquavers.

A semiquaver is written with its tails, but they are often found in groups with a beam across. The presence of semiquavers usually indicates a **fast** passage of music. There are further, shorter notes, with more tails. Demisemiquavers, for instance, last half as long as semiquavers.

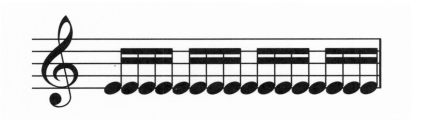

FREE ACCESS on iPhone & Android etc, using any free QR code app

Scan to **HEAR** the C major chord, and access the full library of scales and chords on flametreemusic.com

START HERE

ALL THE BASICS

NOTES & TIMING

PITCH

KEYS

SCALES

COMMON CHORDS

EXTRA NOTATION

Triplets

Triplets are three identical notes tied together to fill the space of **two** equivalent notes.

They are indicated with a 3 above a group of three notes.

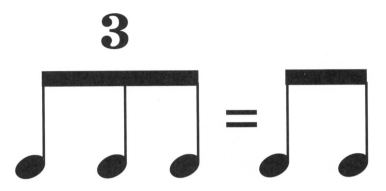

Three **crotchets** grouped as a triplet have the same time value as two crotchets, but **sound faster** because the three notes are played.

Three **quavers** grouped as a triplet have the same time value as two quavers, but sound faster because the three quavers are played.

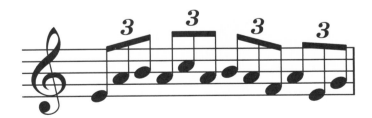

Scan to **HEAR** the C major chord, and access the full library of scales and chords on flametreemusic.com

Dotted Notes

The length of the sound of a note can be increased by one half by adding a single dot to the right-hand side of the notehead.

START
HERE

ALL THE
BASICS

NOTES &
TIMING

PITCH

KEYS

SCALES

COMMON
CHORDS

EXTRA
NOTATION

A **dotted minim** has the same musical length as three crotchets, instead of the usual two, so in a standard musical bar it leaves space for a single crotchet or crotchet rest, as in the example below.

A **dotted crochet** has the same musical length as three quavers. A **dotted quaver** has the same value as three semiquavers.

FREE ACCESS on iPhone & Android etc, using any free QR code app

Scan to **HEAR** the C major chord, and access the full library of scales and chords on flametreemusic.com

Note	Length	Dotted Note	Length
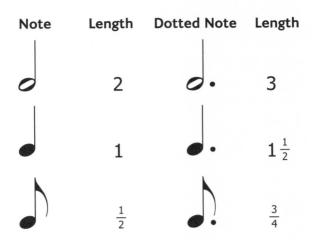

♩ (half note)	2	♩.	3
♩ (quarter note)	1	♩.	$1\frac{1}{2}$
♪ (eighth note)	$\frac{1}{2}$	♪.	$\frac{3}{4}$

mein Herz?

FREE ACCESS on iPhone & Android etc, using any free QR code app

Scan to **HEAR** the C major chord, and access the full library of scales and chords on flametreemusic.com

Ties

Like dotted notes, ties are used to extend the length of a note. Ties are curved lines that connect two notes of the same pitch. The line is drawn from notehead to notehead. The note is only played once, lasting the duration of both the tied notes added together.

Ties are used within a bar to connect two notes where their total value does not have a unique symbol or note. For instance, this is useful for creating the length of a crotchet and a dotted quaver together.

Ties allow a note to be extended **across** a **bar line**.

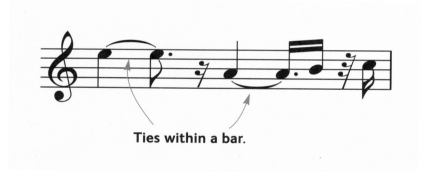

Ties within a bar.

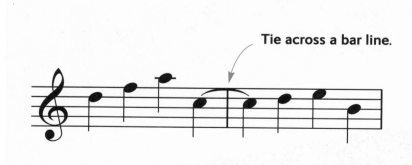

Tie across a bar line.

FREE ACCESS on iPhone & Android
etc, using any free QR code app

Scan to **HEAR** the C major chord, and access the full library of scales and chords on flametreemusic.com

Slurs

Slurs look like ties but they are not the same.

A slur indicates that the music within the start and end points should be played **smoothly**.

A slur connects notes of **different** pitches, and all of them are played.

A slur can **stretch across** several **bars**.

NOTES & TIMING

Rests

For every note there is a corresponding rest.

When looking at a bar of music it is important to realize that each bar must add up to the number of beats set out at the beginning of the piece. Where no notes are to be played, a rest is put in their place to even out the beats.

The look of the rest tells you how long to wait.

START
HERE

ALL THE
BASICS

NOTES &
TIMING

PITCH

KEYS

SCALES

COMMON
CHORDS

EXTRA
NOTATION

FREE ACCESS on iPhone & Android etc, using any free QR code app

Scan to **HEAR** the C major chord, and access the full library of scales and chords on flametreemusic.com

Whole Note/Semibreve Rest

The semibreve rest sits under the fourth line from the bottom line of the stave.

The semibreve rest has the same length as a **semibreve** note.

The standard musical bar contains four beats. A semibreve rest lasts for a **whole bar** of four beats.

If a bar only has three beats, the semibreve rest fills the whole bar too.

Note   Rest

Scan to **HEAR** the C major chord, and access the full library of scales and chords on flametreemusic.com

Half Note/Minim Rest

The minim rest sits on top of the third line from the bottom line of the stave.

The minim rest has the same length as a half note, or **minim**.

The standard musical bar contains four beats.

A minim rest lasts for **half** a **standard bar** and so is equal to two beats.

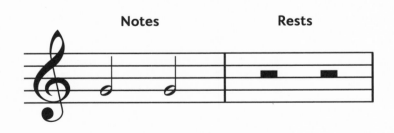

Notes   Rests

FREE ACCESS on iPhone & Android
etc, using any free QR code app

Scan to **HEAR** the C major chord, and
access the full library of scales and
chords on flametreemusic.com

START
HERE

ALL THE
BASICS

NOTES &
TIMING

PITCH

KEYS

SCALES

COMMON
CHORDS

EXTRA
NOTATION

Quarter Note/Crotchet Rest

The crotchet rest is half the length of the minim rest.

It has the same length as a quarter note, or crotchet.

The standard musical bar contains four beats. A crotchet rest lasts for a **quarter** of a **standard bar** and so is equal to one beat.

NOTES & TIMING

Notes   Rests

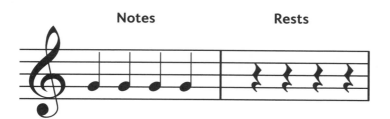

Eighth Note/Quaver Rest

The quaver rest is half the length of the crotchet rest. It has the same length as an eighth note, or quaver.

The standard musical bar contains four beats.

A quaver rest lasts for an **eighth** of a **bar** and so is equal to half a beat.

Notes   Rests

FREE ACCESS on iPhone & Android etc, using any free QR code app

Scan to **HEAR** the C major chord, and access the full library of scales and chords on flametreemusic.com

Sixteenth Note/Semiquaver Rest

The semiquaver rest is half the length of the quaver rest. It has the same length as a sixteenth note, or semiquaver.

The standard musical bar contains four beats.

A semiquaver rest lasts for a **sixteenth** of a **bar** and so has a quarter of a beat.

Notes   Rests

Time Signatures

A time signature tells us how many notes and rests will appear in each bar of music.

The time signature determines the **pulse** of the music: whether it will feel fast or slow.

Time signatures create the framework around which the notes can be written and understood. They organize the sound to help the listener understand what is happening inside the music.

A time signature consists of two numbers:

- The **top** number tells you how many beats there are in each bar.

- The **bottom** number tells you what sort of beat to use:

  - a **2** stands for **half notes (minims)**

  - a **4** stands for **quarter notes (crotchets)**

  - an **8** stands for **eighth notes (quavers)**

The following pages introduce five of the most common time signatures:

$$\frac{4}{4} \quad \frac{2}{2} \quad \frac{2}{4} \quad \frac{3}{4} \quad \frac{6}{8}$$

FREE ACCESS on iPhone & Android etc, using any free QR code app

Scan to **HEAR** the C major chord, and access the full library of scales and chords on flametreemusic.com

START HERE

ALL THE BASICS

NOTES & TIMING

PITCH

KEYS

SCALES

COMMON CHORDS

EXTRA NOTATION

NOTES & TIMING

Scan to **HEAR** the C major chord, and access the full library of scales and chords on flametreemusic.com

Four Quarter Notes Per Bar

The time signature shown with this symbol is four quarter notes/crotchets for each bar.

The **top number** shows that there are **four beats** in every **bar**.

The **bottom** number shows the **length** of each **beat**, in this case **quarter notes/crotchets**.

START
HERE

ALL THE
BASICS

NOTES &
TIMING

PITCH

KEYS

SCALES

COMMON
CHORDS

EXTRA
NOTATION

FREE ACCESS on iPhone & Android
etc, using any free QR code app

Scan to **HEAR** the C major chord, and
access the full library of scales and
chords on flametreemusic.com

Common Time

This symbol is an alternative to the symbol on the opposite page, and represents the same time signature.

The C (which is short for **Common Time**) means **four quarter notes/crotchets** for each **bar**.

There are **four beats** in every **bar**, with each of the four beats being **quarter notes/crotchets**.

Two Half Notes Per Bar

The time signature shown with this symbol represents two half notes/minims for each bar.

The **top number** shows that there are **two beats** in every **bar**.

The **bottom** number shows the **length** of each **beat**, in this case **half notes/minims**.

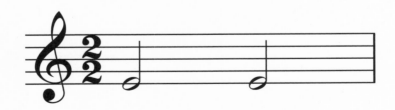

Scan to **HEAR** the C major chord, and access the full library of scales and chords on flametreemusic.com

44

Cut Time

This symbol is an alternative to the symbol on the opposite page, **and represents the same time signature**.

The C (which is short for **Cut Time**) means **two half notes/minims** for each **bar**.

There are **two beats** in every **bar**, with each of the two beats being **half notes/minims**.

NOTES & TIMING

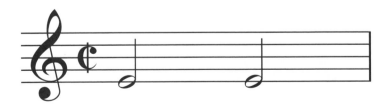

Scan to **HEAR** the C major chord, and access the full library of scales and chords on flametreemusic.com

Two Quarter Notes Per Bar

The time signature shown with this symbol is two quarter notes/crotchets for each bar.

The **top number** shows that there are **two beats** in every **bar**.

The **bottom** number shows the **length** of each **beat**, in this case **quarter notes/crotchets**.

START
HERE

ALL THE
BASICS

NOTES &
TIMING

PITCH

KEYS

SCALES

COMMON
CHORDS

EXTRA
NOTATION

FREE ACCESS on iPhone & Android
etc, using any free QR code app

Scan to **HEAR** the C major chord, and
access the full library of scales and
chords on flametreemusic.com

Three Quarter Notes Per Bar

The time signature shown with this symbol is three quarter notes/crotchets for each bar.

The **top number** shows that there are **three beats** in every **bar**.

The **bottom** number shows the **length** of each **beat**, in this case **quarter notes/crotchets**.

START HERE

ALL THE BASICS

NOTES & TIMING

3

4

PITCH

KEYS

SCALES

COMMON CHORDS

EXTRA NOTATION

FREE ACCESS on iPhone & Android etc, using any free QR code app

Scan to **HEAR** the C major chord, and access the full library of scales and chords on flametreemusic.com

Six Eighth Notes Per Bar

The time signature shown with this symbol is six eighth notes/quavers for each bar.

The **top number** shows that there are **six beats** in every **bar**.

The **bottom** number shows the **length** of each **beat**, in this case, **eighth notes/quavers**.

In this time signature the six notes are grouped in threes.

START
HERE

ALL THE
BASICS

NOTES &
TIMING

PITCH

KEYS

SCALES

COMMON
CHORDS

EXTRA
NOTATION

FREE ACCESS on iPhone & Android
etc, using any free QR code app

Scan to **HEAR** the C major chord, and
access the full library of scales and
chords on flametreemusic.com

FREE ACCESS on iPhone & Android etc, using any free QR code app

Scan to **HEAR** the C major chord, and access the full library of scales and chords on flametreemusic.com

The Treble Clef

How high or low a note is – its pitch – is indicated by where it is positioned on the stave. In standard western music, there are 7 whole note names to describe these positions:

A B C D E F G

The clef tells you which **range of pitches** the notes on the stave represent.

The **treble clef** is used for notes **above middle C**. On the piano this applies generally to the music played with the **right hand**.

Instruments such as the **guitar**, **saxophone**, **trumpet**, **violin** and the **clarinet** also use the treble clef, along with higher voices such as the **soprano** (or treble) sounds of children and female singers.

Scan to **HEAR** the C major chord, and access the full library of scales and chords on flametreemusic.com

START HERE

ALL THE BASICS

NOTES & TIMING

PITCH

KEYS

SCALES

COMMON CHORDS

EXTRA NOTATION

PITCH

FREE ACCESS on iPhone & Android
etc, using any free QR code app

Scan to **HEAR** the C major chord, and
access the full library of scales and
chords on flametreemusic.com

Treble Clef
Line Notes

A good way to remember the names for those notes that appear on the lines of the treble clef is to use a mnemonic to remind you:

START
HERE

ALL THE
BASICS

NOTES &
TIMING

PITCH

KEYS

SCALES

COMMON
CHORDS

EXTRA
NOTATION

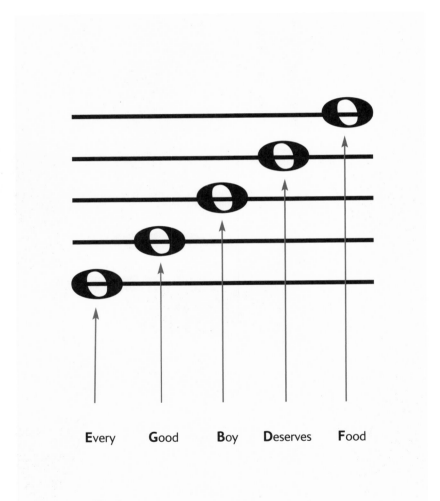

Every   **G**ood   **B**oy   **D**eserves   **F**ood

Scan to **HEAR** the C major chord, and access the full library of scales and chords on flametreemusic.com

Treble Clef
Space Notes

You can use a similar method to remember those notes that appear in the spaces of the treble clef. They spell out a simple word:

PITCH

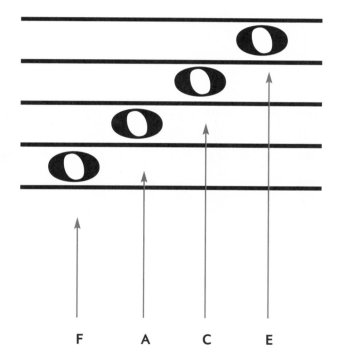

F   A   C   E

Treble Clef Line Notes on the Keyboard

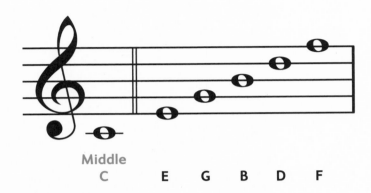

Middle C E G B D F

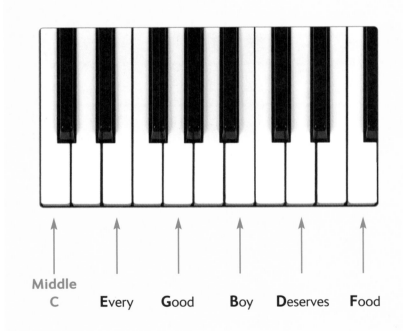

Middle C **E**very **G**ood **B**oy **D**eserves **F**ood

Scan to **HEAR** the C major chord, and access the full library of scales and chords on flametreemusic.com

START HERE

ALL THE BASICS

NOTES & TIMING

PITCH

KEYS

SCALES

COMMON CHORDS

EXTRA NOTATION

Treble Clef Space Notes on the Keyboard

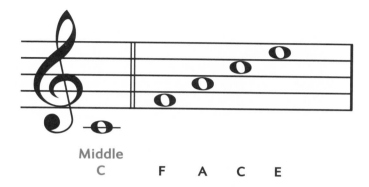

Middle
C   F   A   C   E

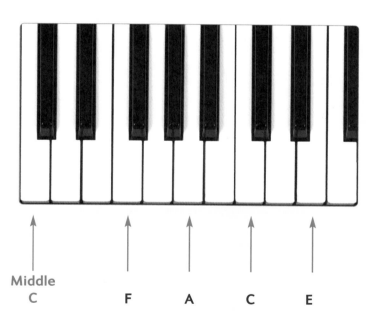

Middle
C   F   A   C   E

FREE ACCESS on iPhone & Android etc, using any free QR code app

Scan to **HEAR** the C major chord, and access the full library of scales and chords on flametreemusic.com

Treble Clef Line Notes on the Guitar

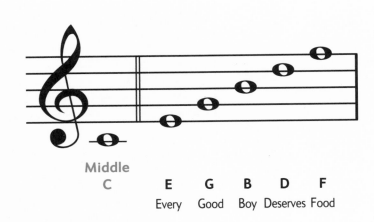

Middle
C   **E**   **G**   **B**   **D**   **F**

Every   Good   Boy   Deserves   Food

START
HERE

ALL THE
BASICS

NOTES &
TIMING

PITCH

KEYS

SCALES

COMMON
CHORDS

EXTRA
NOTATION

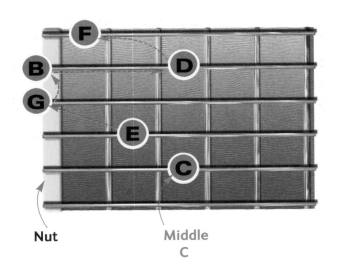

Nut   Middle
C

The diagram here is from the player's view. Treble clef line notes on a guitar are spread across the strings. The notes G and B are shown here on the open strings.

FREE ACCESS on iPhone & Android
etc, using any free QR code app

Scan to **HEAR** the C major chord, and
access the full library of scales and
chords on flametreemusic.com

Treble Clef Space Notes on the Guitar

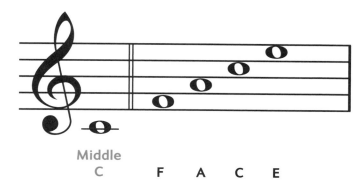

Middle
C   F   A   C   E

START
HERE

ALL THE
BASICS

NOTES &
TIMING

PITCH

KEYS

SCALES

COMMON
CHORDS

EXTRA
NOTATION

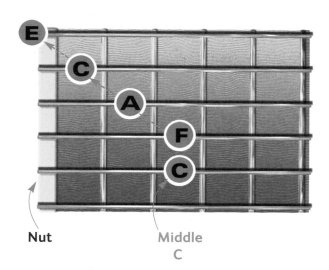

Nut   Middle
C

Again, the diagram here is from the player's view with the treble clef open notes played across the strings. The top note E is shown here on the open string.

FREE ACCESS on iPhone & Android etc, using any free QR code app

Scan to **HEAR** the C major chord, and access the full library of scales and chords on flametreemusic.com

Notes Below the Treble Clef Stave

It is very useful to know how to work out the names of the notes below middle C.

Remember that the **lower** the **position** of the note on the stave, the **lower** the **note**.

Remember also that these notes usually **only** appear on the ledger lines **if** there is **no bass clef**.

However, in piano music, **ledger lines** are sometimes used to signify that the notes should be played by the **right hand**, with the **bass clef** being reserved for the **left hand**.

START
HERE

ALL THE
BASICS

NOTES &
TIMING

PITCH

KEYS

SCALES

COMMON
CHORDS

EXTRA
NOTATION

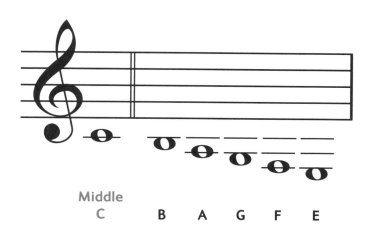

Middle C   B   A   G   F   E

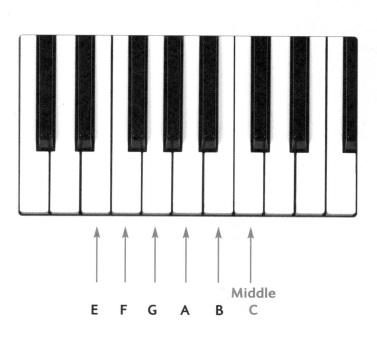

E   F   G   A   B   Middle C

FREE ACCESS on iPhone & Android etc, using any free QR code app

Scan to **HEAR** the C major chord, and access the full library of scales and chords on flametreemusic.com

START HERE

ALL THE BASICS

NOTES & TIMING

PITCH

KEYS

SCALES

COMMON CHORDS

EXTRA NOTATION

Notes Above the Treble Clef Stave

It is also useful to know how to work out the names of the notes above the stave.

Remember that the **higher** the **position** of the note on the stave, the **higher** the **note**.

The notes **above** the stave can be worked out in relation to middle C. For instance, the **A above** the stave can be called the **second A above** middle C.

Scan to **HEAR** the C major chord, and access the full library of scales and chords on flametreemusic.com

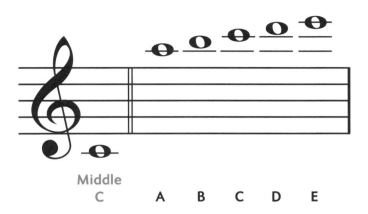

Middle
C   A   B   C   D   E

PITCH

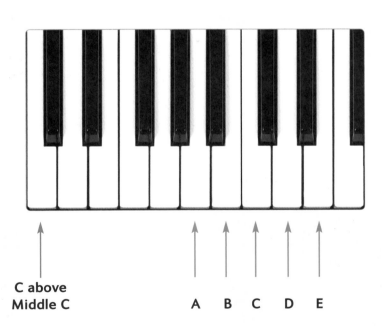

C above
Middle C   A   B   C   D   E

FREE ACCESS on iPhone & Android
etc, using any free QR code app

Scan to **HEAR** the C major chord, and
access the full library of scales and
chords on flametreemusic.com

Octaves

START HERE

ALL THE BASICS

NOTES & TIMING

From the previous pages you might have noticed that the note names appear more than once on a stave. For instance, in the treble clef, in the spaces between the lines, the C of F A C E is above middle C, which sits below the stave.

This occurs because the **7** whole **note names** from **A** to **G** are repeated.

If you listen to the sound of middle C and the sound of the C above, you will hear that they have the same quality. Between notes of the same name, the **interval** – the difference between the two pitches – is called an **octave**. When notes of the same name are played together they create a rich, enhanced sound.

PITCH

KEYS

SCALES

COMMON CHORDS

EXTRA NOTATION

FREE ACCESS on iPhone & Android etc, using any free QR code app

Scan to **HEAR** the C major chord, and access the full library of scales and chords on flametreemusic.com

The interval between the two C notes is an octave.

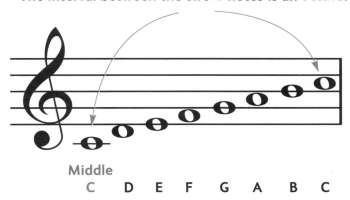

Middle
C   D   E   F   G   A   B   C

Examples of other octaves.

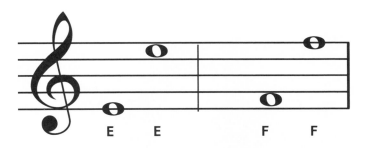

E   E   F   F

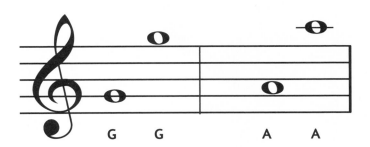

G   G   A   A

Scan to **HEAR** the C major chord, and access the full library of scales and chords on flametreemusic.com

The Bass Clef

The bass clef is used for notes below middle C. On the piano this applies generally to the music played with the left hand.

Instruments such as the **cello**, **bassoon**, **trombone**, **tuba** and the **bass guitar** also use the bass clef, along with lower voices such as the **baritone**, **tenor** and **bass** sounds of adult male singers.

This chapter offers more detailed information on the bass clef and provides ways to remember the notes on the lines and spaces.

FREE ACCESS on iPhone & Android
etc, using any free QR code app

Scan to **HEAR** the C major chord, and access the full library of scales and chords on flametreemusic.com

PITCH

FREE ACCESS on iPhone & Android
etc, using any free QR code app

Scan to **HEAR** the C major chord, and
access the full library of scales and
chords on flametreemusic.com

Bass Clef
Line Notes

As with the treble clef, a good way to remember the names for those notes that appear on the lines of the bass clef is to use a mnemonic to remind you:

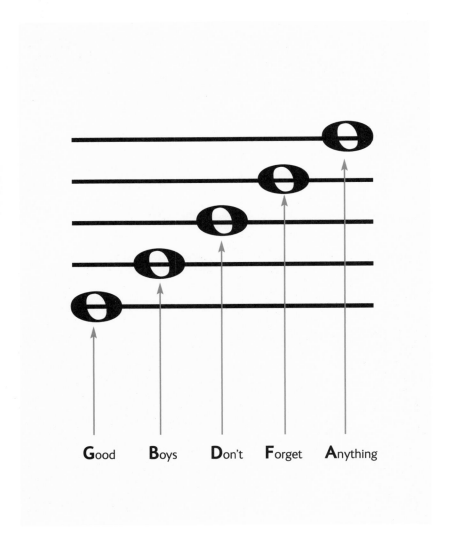

Good **B**oys **D**on't **F**orget **A**nything

Scan to **HEAR** the C major chord, and
access the full library of scales and
chords on flametreemusic.com

START
HERE

ALL THE
BASICS

NOTES &
TIMING

PITCH

KEYS

SCALES

COMMON
CHORDS

EXTRA
NOTATION

Bass Clef
Space Notes

Similarly, you can remember the names for those notes that appear in the spaces of the bass clef stave by using the help of this handy mnemonic:

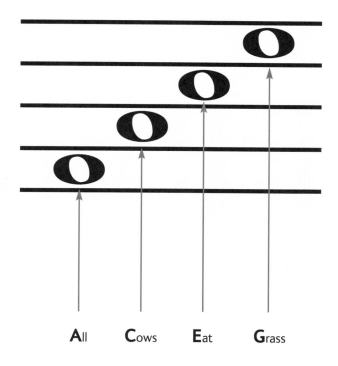

All   **C**ows   **E**at   **G**rass

Scan to **HEAR** the C major chord, and access the full library of scales and chords on flametreemusic.com

START HERE

ALL THE BASICS

NOTES & TIMING

PITCH

KEYS

SCALES

COMMON CHORDS

EXTRA NOTATION

Bass Clef Line Notes on the Keyboard

START
HERE

ALL THE
BASICS

NOTES &
TIMING

PITCH

KEYS

SCALES

COMMON
CHORDS

EXTRA
NOTATION

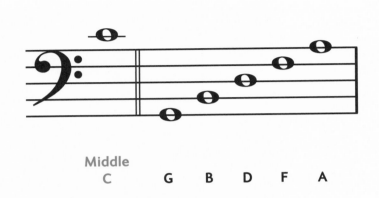

Middle
C   G   B   D   F   A

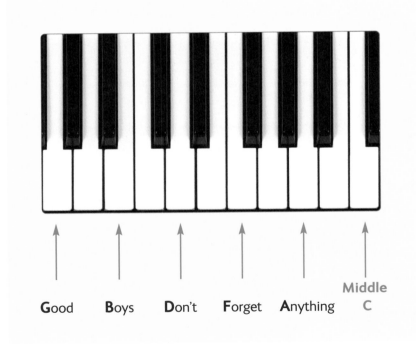

Good   **B**oys   **D**on't   **F**orget   **A**nything   Middle **C**

FREE ACCESS on iPhone & Android
etc, using any free QR code app

Scan to **HEAR** the C major chord, and
access the full library of scales and
chords on flametreemusic.com

Bass Clef Space Notes
on the Keyboard

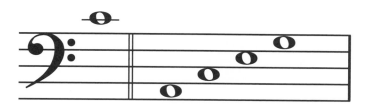

Middle
C   A   C   E   G

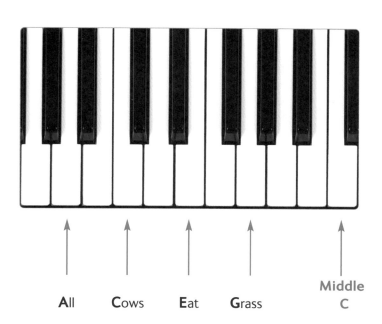

All   **C**ows   **E**at   **G**rass   Middle
C

FREE ACCESS on iPhone & Android
etc, using any free QR code app

Scan to **HEAR** the C major chord, and
access the full library of scales and
chords on flametreemusic.com

Bass Clef Line Notes
on the Bass Guitar

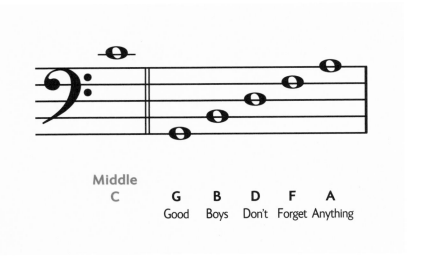

Middle C	G	B	D	F	A
	Good	Boys	Don't	Forget	Anything

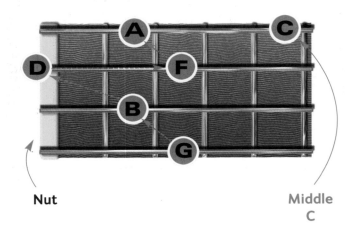

Nut   Middle
                                                   C

The diagram here is from the player's view. Bass clef line notes on a bass guitar are spread across the strings. The note D is shown on the open string.

FREE ACCESS on iPhone & Android
etc, using any free QR code app

Scan to **HEAR** the C major chord, and access the full library of scales and chords on flametreemusic.com

Bass Clef Space Notes
on the Bass Guitar

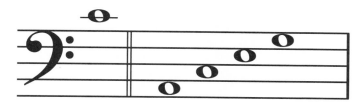

Middle
C

A	C	E	G
All	Cows	Eat	Grass

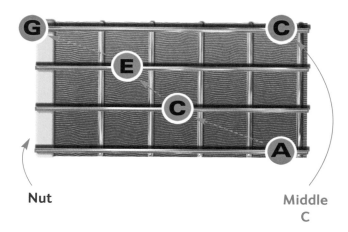

Nut

Middle
C

The diagram here is from the player's view. Bass clef line notes
on a bass guitar are spread across the strings. The note G is
shown on the open string.

FREE ACCESS on iPhone & Android
etc, using any free QR code app

Scan to **HEAR** the C major chord, and
access the full library of scales and
chords on flametreemusic.com

Notes Below the Bass Clef Stave

It is very useful to know how to work out the names of the notes below middle C.

Remember that the **lower** the **position** of the note on the stave, the **lower** the **note**.

As a guide, a **cello** would normally only make notes as low as the C two octaves below middle C.

START HERE

ALL THE BASICS

NOTES & TIMING

PITCH

KEYS

SCALES

COMMON CHORDS

EXTRA NOTATION

FREE ACCESS on iPhone & Android etc, using any free QR code app

Scan to **HEAR** the C major chord, and access the full library of scales and chords on flametreemusic.com

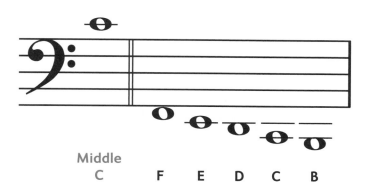

Middle
C   F   E   D   C   B

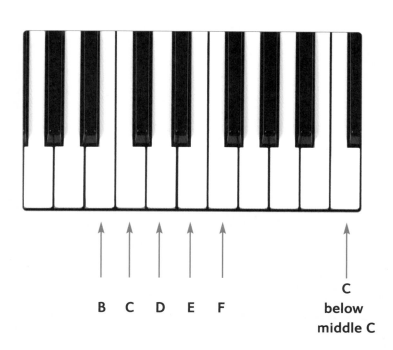

B   C   D   E   F   C
below
middle C

FREE ACCESS on iPhone & Android
etc, using any free QR code app

Scan to **HEAR** the C major chord, and
access the full library of scales and
chords on flametreemusic.com

PITCH

Notes Above the Bass Clef Stave

It is also useful to know how to work out the names of the notes above the stave.

Remember that the **higher** the **position** of the note on the stave, the **higher** the **note**.

The notes **above** the stave can be worked out in relation to middle C.

Remember, the ledger lines only apply where no treble clef is used, or, on the piano, to show that a note should be played with the left hand. The **G** opposite is normally the **highest note** played by a double bass or bass guitar.

START
HERE

ALL THE
BASICS

NOTES &
TIMING

PITCH

KEYS

SCALES

COMMON
CHORDS

EXTRA
NOTATION

FREE ACCESS on iPhone & Android
etc, using any free QR code app

Scan to **HEAR** the C major chord, and access the full library of scales and chords on flametreemusic.com

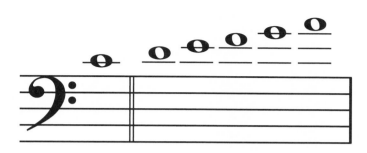

Middle
C   D   E   F   G   A

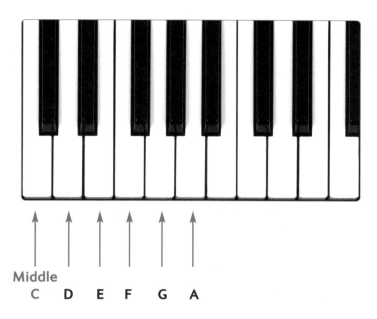

Middle
C   D   E   F   G   A

START HERE

ALL THE BASICS

NOTES & TIMING

PITCH

KEYS

SCALES

COMMON CHORDS

EXTRA NOTATION

FREE ACCESS on iPhone & Android
etc, using any free QR code app

Scan to **HEAR** the C major chord, and
access the full library of scales and
chords on flametreemusic.com

START
HERE

ALL THE
BASICS

NOTES &
TIMING

PITCH

KEYS

SCALES

COMMON
CHORDS

EXTRA
NOTATION

Sharps, Flats & Naturals

The notes we've covered so far in this book have been natural notes. They are played on the white notes of a piano and have the following names:

A B C D E F G

However, there are notes that sit between some of these whole notes. These notes are indicated by a **sharp** or a **flat**. They are called **accidentals** when they are outside the key of the music (see pages 88–103 for more on keys). On the piano, they are played on the **black** keys. The difference in pitch – the **interval** – between a white key and the black one it sits next to is half a tone (a **semitone**).

A **natural** sign is used to cancel out a flat or sharp, returning the note to its 'natural state'.

On the Keyboard

You can see here how the 12 notes work before they are repeated. For clarity at this stage the diagrams opposite just use sharp signs, although later we will look at flat signs too.

Enharmonic Equivalents

Enharmonic equivalents are notes that sound the same, but are represented with a different 'spelling' in music notation. For example, all the black keys on the piano can be described as 'sharp' notes, but they also can be described in terms of 'flats'. The following pages will help to clarify this relationship.

FREE ACCESS on iPhone & Android etc, using any free QR code app

Scan to **HEAR** the C major chord, and access the full library of scales and chords on flametreemusic.com

C C♯ D D♯ E F F♯ G G♯ A A♯ B

Natural notes on the white keys, sharp (or flat) notes on the black keys

C D E F G A B C

C♯ D♯ F♯ G♯ A♯

START HERE

ALL THE BASICS

NOTES & TIMING

PITCH

KEYS

SCALES

COMMON CHORDS

EXTRA NOTATION

FREE ACCESS on iPhone & Android etc, using any free QR code app

Scan to **HEAR** the C major chord, and access the full library of scales and chords on flametreemusic.com

Sharps

This is the sharp sign.

It is written to the **left** of a notehead.

A **sharpened** note is half a tone **higher** than the note that is being sharpened.

When a sharp is written in front of a particular note all **subsequent uses** of that note **in the bar** will also be **sharpened**. From the beginning of the next bar, the note reverts to its previous state.

Sharpened notes are played on the **black** keys of a piano.

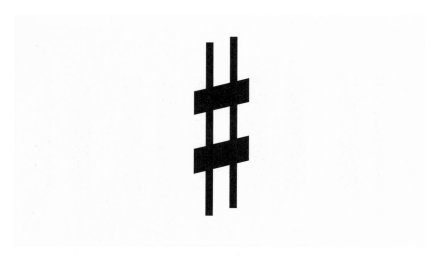

START
HERE

ALL THE
BASICS

NOTES &
TIMING

PITCH

KEYS

SCALES

COMMON
CHORDS

EXTRA
NOTATION

Flats

This is the flat sign.

It is written to the **left** of a notehead.

A **flattened** note is half a tone **lower** than the note that is being flattened.

When a flat is written in front of a particular note all **subsequent uses** of that note **in the bar** will also be **flattened**. From the beginning of the next bar, the note reverts to its previous state.

Flattened notes are played on the **black** keys of a piano.

START
HERE

ALL THE
BASICS

NOTES &
TIMING

PITCH

KEYS

SCALES

COMMON
CHORDS

EXTRA
NOTATION

FREE ACCESS on iPhone & Android
etc, using any free QR code app

Scan to **HEAR** the C major chord, and access the full library of scales and chords on flametreemusic.com

Sharp and Flat Notes on the Keyboard

Sharp and flat notes appear on the black keys on the piano.

Remember, **sharp** notes describe sounds that are a semitone **higher** than the natural note, and **flat** notes describe sounds a semitone **lower**.

For example, C# is a semitone higher than C, and D♭ is a semitone lower than D.

On the diagram opposite, you can see that both of these describe **the same black note**: so D♭ is an **enharmonic equivalent** of C#. In this way, every sharpened note has an equivalent 'flat' name.

You can also see there are **no black keys** between B and C, or between E and F.

So 'B#' refers to the same note as C, and E# refers to the same note as F.

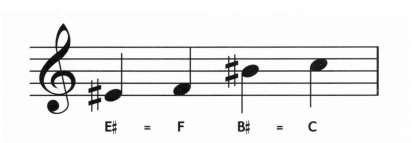

E# = F   B# = C

Equally, F♭ refers to the same note as E, and C♭ refers to the same note as B.

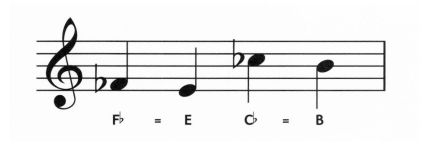

F♭ = E   C♭ = B

FREE ACCESS on iPhone & Android etc, using any free QR code app

Scan to **HEAR** the C major chord, and access the full library of scales and chords on flametreemusic.com

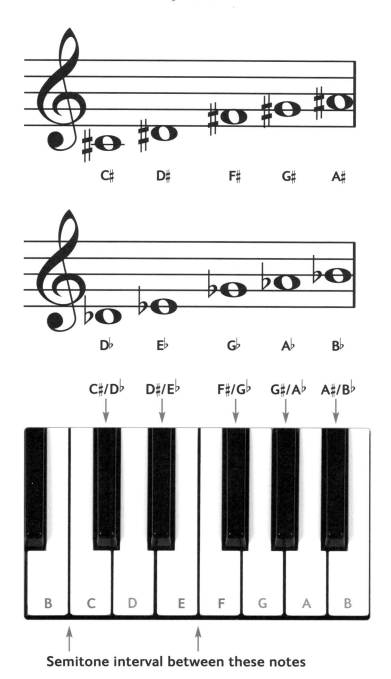

C# D# F# G# A#

D♭ E♭ G♭ A♭ B♭

C#/D♭ D#/E♭ F#/G♭ G#/A♭ A#/B♭

PITCH

B C D E F G A B

Semitone interval between these notes

FREE ACCESS on iPhone & Android
etc, using any free QR code app

Scan to **HEAR** the C major chord, and
access the full library of scales and
chords on flametreemusic.com

Sharp and Flat Notes on the Guitar

On the guitar, the frets are organized in semitone intervals.

Sharp notes appear **after** their natural note, as they are a semitone **higher**.

Flat notes appear **before** their natural note, as they are a semitone **lower**.

The below diagram shows the sharp and flat notes as they appear alongside the **natural** notes on the guitar.

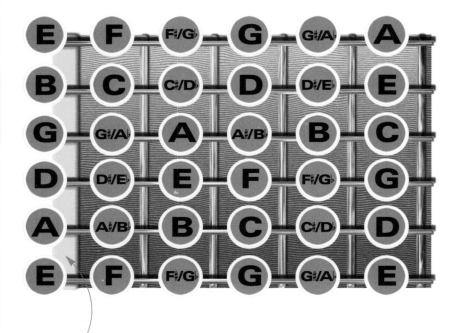

Nut

Player's view. Bass notes at the bottom.

FREE ACCESS on iPhone & Android etc, using any free QR code app

Scan to **HEAR** the C major chord, and access the full library of scales and chords on flametreemusic.com

As a reminder, these are the **sharp** notes in the octave above middle C:

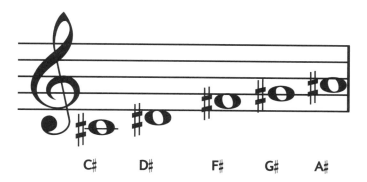

C♯   D♯   F♯   G♯   A♯

And these are the **flat** notes in the octave above middle C:

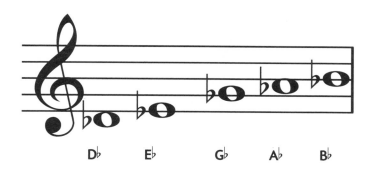

D♭   E♭   G♭   A♭   B♭

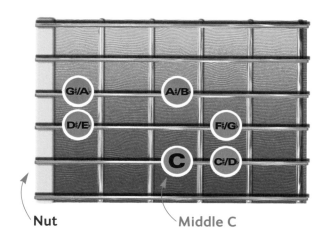

Nut   Middle C

Scan to **HEAR** the C major chord, and access the full library of scales and chords on flametreemusic.com

Naturals

This is the natural sign.

It is written to the **left** of a notehead.

A natural sign is used to **cancel** the effect of a **sharp** or a **flat** note played previously in the same bar, or present in the key signature (see page 88).

Natural notes are played on the **white** keys of a piano.

FREE ACCESS on iPhone & Android etc, using any free QR code app

Scan to **HEAR** the C major chord, and access the full library of scales and chords on flametreemusic.com

START
HERE

ALL THE
BASICS

NOTES &
TIMING

PITCH

KEYS

SCALES

COMMON
CHORDS

EXTRA
NOTATION

Notes with a natural symbol occur when a particular note has been sharpened or flattened previously in the bar or in the key signature.

Once applied, the **natural** symbol for the particular note applies for the rest of the bar unless another sharp or flat appears.

A **D♯** is a **semitone** higher than **D♮**.

A **D♭** is a **semitone** lower than **D♮**.

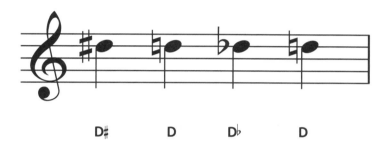

D♯   D   D♭   D

PITCH

FREE ACCESS on iPhone & Android etc, using any free QR code app

Scan to **HEAR** the C major chord, and access the full library of scales and chords on flametreemusic.com

Natural Notes on the Keyboard

Here is a reminder of the natural notes on the keyboard.
A natural sign restores any sharpened or flattened note to its
natural state.

START
HERE

ALL THE
BASICS

NOTES &
TIMING

PITCH

KEYS

SCALES

COMMON
CHORDS

EXTRA
NOTATION

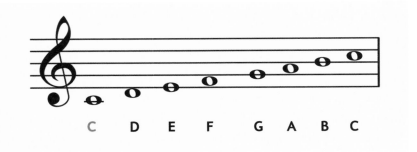

C   D   E   F   G   A   B   C

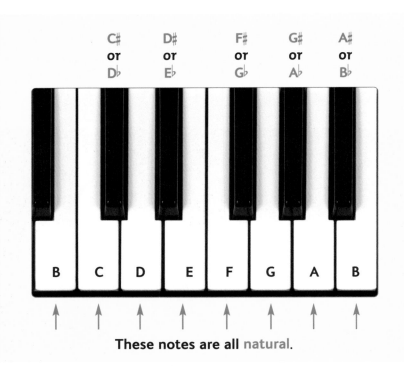

These notes are all natural.

FREE ACCESS on iPhone & Android
etc, using any free QR code app

Scan to **HEAR** the C major chord, and
access the full library of scales and
chords on flametreemusic.com

Natural Notes on the Guitar

Notes in TAB are shown on six lines representing the six strings of the guitar.

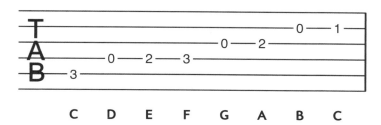

The low E string is at the bottom and the notes are given the fret number on the appropriate string. The natural notes are shown in TAB above and a guitar diagram below.

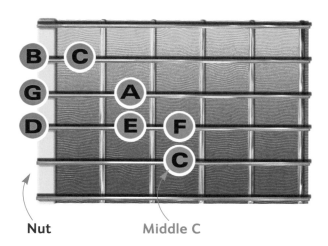

Nut   Middle C

FREE ACCESS on iPhone & Android etc, using any free QR code app

Scan to **HEAR** the C major chord, and access the full library of scales and chords on flametreemusic.com

START HERE

ALL THE BASICS

NOTES & TIMING

PITCH

KEYS

SCALES

COMMON CHORDS

EXTRA NOTATION

Key Signatures

START
HERE

ALL THE
BASICS

NOTES &
TIMING

PITCH

KEYS

SCALES

COMMON
CHORDS

EXTRA
NOTATION

The natural notes above and below middle C are the white keys on a piano. Key signatures allow us to use the black notes, which are the sharps and flats.

A sharp or flat in the **key signature** indicates that these should be played each time the note appears. Each key signature contains a different number of either sharps or flats (never both) and makes the music sound distinctive.

A key signature is shown at the **start** of each stave – after the clef, before the time signature – and is indicated by sharp or flat symbols on note lines or spaces.

Accidentals are any sharps or flats that appear in the music but are not part of the key signature. If enough of the same accidentals appear, it could be a sign that the music is changing key.

The following pages will show how all the different key signatures are represented in sheet music.

Relative Minors

Each major key corresponds with a minor key that shares the **same** key signature. These are known as '**relatives**'.

Relative keys are closely linked, with the main shift of emphasis being that they have a different **tonal centre**, or **key note**. For example, G major and E minor are relative keys, but G major and G minor are simply **versions** of each other. The **sixth** note of a major scale tells you the key note of its relative minor: so the relative of C major is A minor (see pages 104–55 for scales).

No Sharps or Flats

C Major

A Minor

The keys of C major and its relative, A minor, have no sharps or flats. If any section of music in C major or A minor contains sharps or flats, these are accidentals.

START
HERE

ALL THE
BASICS

NOTES &
TIMING

PITCH

KEYS

SCALES

COMMON
CHORDS

EXTRA
NOTATION

FREE ACCESS on iPhone & Android etc, using any free QR code app

Scan to **HEAR** the C major chord, and access the full library of scales and chords on flametreemusic.com

1 Sharp

G Major

E Minor

The keys of G major and its relative, E minor, have one sharp:

FREE ACCESS on iPhone & Android etc, using any free QR code app

Scan to **HEAR** the C major chord, and access the full library of scales and chords on flametreemusic.com

1 Flat

F Major

D Minor

The keys of F major and its relative, D minor, have one flat:

START HERE

ALL THE BASICS

NOTES & TIMING

PITCH

KEYS

SCALES

COMMON CHORDS

EXTRA NOTATION

FREE ACCESS on iPhone & Android etc, using any free QR code app

Scan to **HEAR** the C major chord, and access the full library of scales and chords on flametreemusic.com

91

2 Sharps
D Major
B Minor

The keys of D major and its relative, B minor, have two sharps:

FREE ACCESS on iPhone & Android etc, using any free QR code app

Scan to **HEAR** the C major chord, and access the full library of scales and chords on flametreemusic.com

START HERE

ALL THE BASICS

NOTES & TIMING

PITCH

KEYS

SCALES

COMMON CHORDS

EXTRA NOTATION

2 Flats

B♭ Major

G Minor

The keys of B♭major and its relative, G minor, have two flats:

B♭ E♭

FREE ACCESS on iPhone & Android etc, using any free QR code app

Scan to **HEAR** the C major chord, and access the full library of scales and chords on flametreemusic.com

START
HERE

ALL THE
BASICS

NOTES &
TIMING

PITCH

KEYS

SCALES

COMMON
CHORDS

EXTRA
NOTATION

3 Sharps

A Major

F# Minor

**The keys of A major and its relative,
F# minor, have three sharps:**

F# C# G#

FREE ACCESS on iPhone & Android
etc, using any free QR code app

Scan to **HEAR** the C major chord, and
access the full library of scales and
chords on flametreemusic.com

94

3 Flats

E♭ Major

C Minor

The keys of E♭ major and its relative, C minor, have three flats:

START HERE

ALL THE BASICS

NOTES & TIMING

PITCH

KEYS

SCALES

COMMON CHORDS

EXTRA NOTATION

FREE ACCESS on iPhone & Android etc, using any free QR code app

Scan to **HEAR** the C major chord, and access the full library of scales and chords on flametreemusic.com

4 Sharps

E Major

C# Minor

The keys of E major and its relative, C# minor, have four sharps:

START HERE
ALL THE BASICS
NOTES & TIMING
PITCH
KEYS
SCALES
COMMON CHORDS
EXTRA NOTATION

FREE ACCESS on iPhone & Android etc, using any free QR code app

Scan to **HEAR** the C major chord, and access the full library of scales and chords on flametreemusic.com

4 Flats

A♭ Major

F Minor

The keys of A♭ major and its relative, F minor, have four flats:

B♭ E♭ A♭ D♭

KEYS

Scan to **HEAR** the C major chord, and access the full library of scales and chords on flametreemusic.com

5 Sharps

B Major

G♯ Minor

The keys of B major and its relative, G# minor, have five sharps:

F♯ C♯ G♯ D♯ A♯

FREE ACCESS on iPhone & Android etc, using any free QR code app

Scan to **HEAR** the C major chord, and access the full library of scales and chords on flametreemusic.com

START HERE

ALL THE BASICS

NOTES & TIMING

PITCH

KEYS

SCALES

COMMON CHORDS

EXTRA NOTATION

5 Flats

D♭ Major

B♭ Minor

The keys of D♭ major and its relative, B♭ minor, have five flats:

START HERE

ALL THE BASICS

NOTES & TIMING

PITCH

KEYS

SCALES

COMMON CHORDS

EXTRA NOTATION

FREE ACCESS on iPhone & Android etc, using any free QR code app

Scan to **HEAR** the C major chord, and access the full library of scales and chords on flametreemusic.com

START
HERE

ALL THE
BASICS

NOTES &
TIMING

PITCH

KEYS

SCALES

COMMON
CHORDS

EXTRA
NOTATION

6 Sharps
F# Major
D# Minor

**The keys of F# major and its relative,
D# minor, have six sharps:**

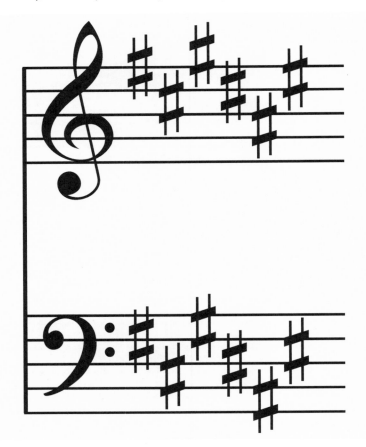

FREE ACCESS on iPhone & Android
etc, using any free QR code app

Scan to **HEAR** the C major chord, and
access the full library of scales and
chords on flametreemusic.com

6 Flats

G♭ Major

E♭ Minor

**The keys of G♭ major and its relative,
E♭ minor, have six flats:**

START
HERE

ALL THE
BASICS

NOTES &
TIMING

PITCH

KEYS

SCALES

COMMON
CHORDS

EXTRA
NOTATION

FREE ACCESS on iPhone & Android
etc, using any free QR code app

Scan to **HEAR** the C major chord, and
access the full library of scales and
chords on flametreemusic.com

7 Sharps

C♯ Major

A♯ Minor

**The keys of C♯ major and its relative,
A♯ minor, have seven sharps:**

F♯ C♯ G♯ D♯ A♯ E♯ B♯

START HERE

ALL THE BASICS

NOTES & TIMING

PITCH

KEYS

SCALES

COMMON CHORDS

EXTRA NOTATION

FREE ACCESS on iPhone & Android
etc, using any free QR code app

Scan to **HEAR** the C major chord, and
access the full library of scales and
chords on flametreemusic.com

7 Flats

C♭ Major

A♭ Minor

**The keys of C♭ major and its relative,
A♭ minor, have seven flats:**

B♭ E♭ A♭ D♭ G♭ C♭ F♭

KEYS

FREE ACCESS on iPhone & Android
etc, using any free QR code app

Scan to **HEAR** the C major chord, and
access the full library of scales and
chords on flametreemusic.com

Scales

Scales are rising and falling notes organized according to a particular pattern. All key signatures have major and minor scales associated with them, but there are other scales that allow further expression and are suitable for different types of music.

In this section we look at four scales per note: **major**, **natural minor**, **harmonic minor** and melodic minor. They each have a distinctive pattern that makes them suitable for a range of musical styles.

Learning the relationship of notes in a particular scale will help you spot when a piece is **changing key** and improve your understanding of music as a whole.

START
HERE

ALL THE
BASICS

NOTES &
TIMING

PITCH

KEYS

SCALES

COMMON
CHORDS

EXTRA
NOTATION

FREE ACCESS on iPhone & Android etc, using any free QR code app

Scan to **HEAR** the C major chord, and access the full library of scales and chords on flametreemusic.com

Chromatic Scale

The simplest scale is the chromatic scale because it contains every note from the start to the end of an octave.

Every step of the scale is a **half tone**, or semitone.

Using middle C as the starting point, the C chromatic scale on the keyboard uses **every white** and **every black key** from C to the next C above.

The chromatic scale for every key works in the same way, taking in all the white and black keys, from the starting note of the key to the octave above.

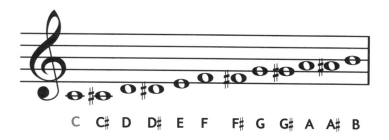

C C♯ D D♯ E F F♯ G G♯ A A♯ B

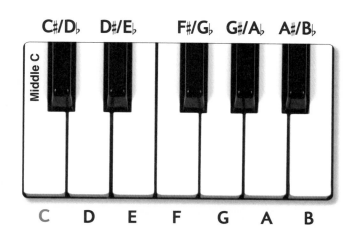

C♯/D♭   D♯/E♭   F♯/G♭ G♯/A♭ A♯/B♭

Middle C

C   D   E   F   G   A   B

Scan to **HEAR** the C major chord, and access the full library of scales and chords on flametreemusic.com

Scale Patterns

This section show four scales for each note. Each scale conforms to a standard pattern, from the root note of the scale.

S = semitone (half step)
T = tone (whole step)
m3 = minor 3rd (three semitones)

Major scale

T T S T T T S

Natural Minor

T S T T S T T

Harmonic Minor

T S T T S m3 S

FREE ACCESS on iPhone & Android
etc, using any free QR code app

Scan to **HEAR** the C major chord, and access the full library of scales and chords on flametreemusic.com

Melodic Minor

T S T T T S

(ascending form only)

The descending form of the melodic minor scale is the same as the natural minor scale.

The following pages show the traditional and TAB notation of these scale variations in all keys.

You can refer to these to understand the key transitions and changes of tone in a piece of music – look for the dominant set of notes that are involved. Being able to recognize the relationship between notes will improve your playing technique as well as give you the knowledge to compose your own music.

Other Types of Scales

Especially common in Guitar music, Pentatonic scales only consist of 5 notes (instead of 7), and are a quick and simple way of achieving a distinct sound. They are often used in Blues music, and follow these patterns:

SCALES

Major Pentatonic: T T m3 T m3
Minor Pentatonic: m3 T T m3 T

See and hear examples of these on our website: flametreemusic.com. Furthermore, each QR code at the bottom of the pages in this section will bring you to the specific scale on flametreemusic.com.

FREE ACCESS on iPhone & Android etc, using any free QR code app

Scan to **HEAR** the C major chord, and access the full library of scales and chords on flametreemusic.com

A B C D E F G

C Major

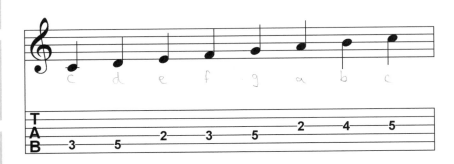

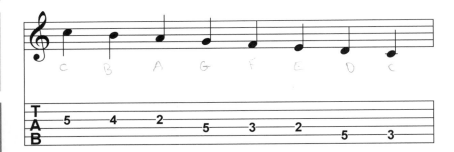

Scale notes	Up	C D E F G A B C
	Down	C B A G F E D C

START HERE

ALL THE BASICS

NOTES & TIMING

PITCH

KEYS

SCALES

COMMON CHORDS

EXTRA NOTATION

FREE ACCESS on iPhone & Android etc, using any free QR code app

Scan to **HEAR** this scale, or go directly to flametreemusic.com

C Natural Minor

START HERE

ALL THE BASICS

NOTES & TIMING

PITCH

KEYS SIGNATURE

SCALES

COMMON CHORDS

EXTRA NOTATION

Scale notes	Up	C D E♭ F G A♭ B♭ C
	Down	C B♭ A♭ G F E♭ D C

FREE ACCESS on iPhone & Android etc, using any free QR code app

Scan to **HEAR** this scale, or go directly to flametreemusic.com

START
HERE

ALL THE
BASICS

NOTES &
TIMING

PITCH

KEYS

SCALES

COMMON
CHORDS

EXTRA
NOTATION

C Harmonic Minor

Scale notes	Up	C D E♭ F G A♭ B C
	Down	C B A♭ G F E♭ D C

FREE ACCESS on iPhone & Android
etc, using any free QR code app

Scan to **HEAR** this scale, or go directly
to flametreemusic.com

110

C Melodic Minor

START
HERE

ALL THE
BASICS

NOTES &
TIMING

PITCH

KEYS
SIGNATURE

SCALES

COMMON
CHORDS

EXTRA
NOTATION

Scale notes	Up	C D E♭ F G A B C
	Down	C B♭ A♭ G F E♭ D C

FREE ACCESS on iPhone & Android etc, using any free QR code app

Scan to **HEAR** this scale, or go directly to flametreemusic.com

START
HERE

ALL THE
BASICS

NOTES &
TIMING

PITCH

KEYS

SCALES

COMMON
CHORDS

EXTRA
NOTATION

D♭ Major

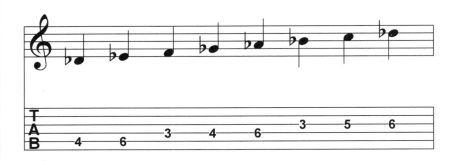

Scale notes	Up	D♭ E♭ F G♭ A♭ B♭ C D♭
	Down	D♭ C B♭ A♭ G♭ F E♭ D♭

Scan to **HEAR** this scale, or go directly
to flametreemusic.com

C♯ Natural Minor

START HERE

ALL THE BASICS

NOTES & TIMING

PITCH

KEYS SIGNATURE

SCALES

COMMON CHORDS

EXTRA NOTATION

Scale notes	Up	C♯ D♯ E F♯ G♯ A B C♯
	Down	C♯ B A G♯ F♯ E D♯ C♯

FREE ACCESS on iPhone & Android etc, using any free QR code app

Scan to **HEAR** this scale, or go directly to flametreemusic.com

START HERE

ALL THE BASICS

NOTES & TIMING

PITCH

KEYS

SCALES

COMMON CHORDS

EXTRA NOTATION

C♯ Harmonic Minor

Scale notes	Up	C♯ D♯ E F♯ G♯ A B♯ C♯
	Down	C♯ B♯ A G♯ F♯ E D♯ C♯

FREE ACCESS on iPhone & Android etc, using any free QR code app

Scan to **HEAR** this scale, or go directly to flametreemusic.com

114

C# Melodic Minor

Scale notes		
	Up	C# D# E F# G# A# B# C#
	Down	C# B♮ A♮ G# F# E D# C#

START
HERE

ALL THE
BASICS

NOTES &
TIMING

PITCH

KEYS
SIGNATURE

SCALES

COMMON
CHORDS

EXTRA
NOTATION

FREE ACCESS on iPhone & Android etc, using any free QR code app

Scan to **HEAR** this scale, or go directly to flametreemusic.com

D Major

START
HERE

ALL THE
BASICS

NOTES &
TIMING

PITCH

KEYS

SCALES

COMMON
CHORDS

EXTRA
NOTATION

Scale notes	Up	D E F♯ G A B C♯ D
	Down	D C♯ B A G F♯ E D

FREE ACCESS on iPhone & Android etc, using any free QR code app

Scan to **HEAR** this scale, or go directly to flametreemusic.com

D Natural Minor

START HERE

ALL THE BASICS

NOTES & TIMING

PITCH

KEYS SIGNATURE

SCALES

COMMON CHORDS

EXTRA NOTATION

Scale notes		
	Up	D E F G A B♭ C D
	Down	D C B♭ A G F E D

FREE ACCESS on iPhone & Android etc, using any free QR code app

Scan to **HEAR** this scale, or go directly to flametreemusic.com

START
HERE

ALL THE
BASICS

NOTES &
TIMING

PITCH

KEYS

SCALES

COMMON
CHORDS

EXTRA
NOTATION

D Harmonic Minor

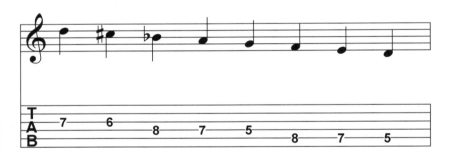

Scale notes		
	Up	D E F G A B♭ C♯ D
	Down	D C♯ B♭ A G F E D

FREE ACCESS on iPhone & Android
etc, using any free QR code app

Scan to **HEAR** this scale, or go directly
to flametreemusic.com

D Melodic Minor

Scale notes	Up	D E F G A B C♯ D
	Down	D C♮ B♭ A G F E D

START HERE

ALL THE BASICS

NOTES & TIMING

PITCH

KEYS SIGNATURE

SCALES

COMMON CHORDS

EXTRA NOTATION

E♭ Major

| Scale notes | Up | E♭ F G A♭ B♭ C D E♭ |
| | Down | E♭ D C B♭ A♭ G F E♭ |

FREE ACCESS on iPhone & Android
etc, using any free QR code app

Scan to **HEAR** this scale, or go directly
to flametreemusic.com

START
HERE

ALL THE
BASICS

NOTES &
TIMING

PITCH

KEYS

SCALES

COMMON
CHORDS

EXTRA
NOTATION

E♭ Natural Minor

Scale notes	Up	E♭ F G♭ A♭ B♭ C♭ D♭ E♭
	Down	E♭ D♭ C♭ B♭ A♭ G♭ F E♭

START HERE

ALL THE BASICS

NOTES & TIMING

PITCH

KEYS SIGNATURE

SCALES

COMMON CHORDS

EXTRA NOTATION

FREE ACCESS on iPhone & Android etc, using any free QR code app

Scan to **HEAR** this scale, or go directly to flametreemusic.com

121

E♭ Harmonic Minor

START
HERE

ALL THE
BASICS

NOTES &
TIMING

PITCH

KEYS

SCALES

COMMON
CHORDS

EXTRA
NOTATION

Scale notes	Up	E♭ F G♭ A♭ B♭ C♭ D E♭
	Down	E♭ D C♭ B♭ A♭ G♭ F E♭

FREE ACCESS on iPhone & Android
etc, using any free QR code app

Scan to **HEAR** this scale, or go directly
to flametreemusic.com

E♭ Melodic Minor

Scale notes	Up	E♭ F G♭ A♭ B♭ C D E♭
	Down	E♭ D♭ C♭ B♭ A♭ G♭ F E♭

START HERE

ALL THE BASICS

NOTES & TIMING

PITCH

KEYS SIGNATURE

SCALES

COMMON CHORDS

EXTRA NOTATION

FREE ACCESS on iPhone & Android etc, using any free QR code app

Scan to **HEAR** this scale, or go directly to flametreemusic.com

123

E Major

START
HERE

ALL THE
BASICS

NOTES &
TIMING

PITCH

KEYS

SCALES

COMMON
CHORDS

EXTRA
NOTATION

Scale notes	Up	E F# G# A B C# D# E
	Down	E D# C# B A G# F# E

FREE ACCESS on iPhone & Android
etc, using any free QR code app

Scan to **HEAR** this scale, or go directly
to flametreemusic.com

E Natural Minor

START HERE

ALL THE BASICS

NOTES & TIMING

PITCH

KEYS SIGNATURE

SCALES

COMMON CHORDS

EXTRA NOTATION

Scale notes	Up	E F♯ G A B C D E
	Down	E D C B A G F♯ E

FREE ACCESS on iPhone & Android etc, using any free QR code app

Scan to **HEAR** this scale, or go directly to flametreemusic.com

125

START
HERE

ALL THE
BASICS

NOTES &
TIMING

PITCH

KEYS

SCALES

COMMON
CHORDS

EXTRA
NOTATION

E Harmonic Minor

Scale notes	Up	E F♯ G A B C D♯ E
	Down	E D♯ C B A G F♯ E

FREE ACCESS on iPhone & Android
etc, using any free QR code app

Scan to **HEAR** this scale, or go directly
to flametreemusic.com

E Melodic Minor

Scale notes	Up	E F# G A B C# D# E
	Down	E D♮ C♮ B A G F# E

Scan to **HEAR** this scale, or go directly to flametreemusic.com

START HERE

ALL THE BASICS

NOTES & TIMING

PITCH

KEYS SIGNATURE

SCALES

COMMON CHORDS

EXTRA NOTATION

F Major

START HERE

ALL THE BASICS

NOTES & TIMING

PITCH

KEYS

SCALES

COMMON CHORDS

EXTRA NOTATION

Scale notes	Up	F G A B♭ C D E F
	Down	F E D C B♭ A G F

FREE ACCESS on iPhone & Android etc, using any free QR code app

Scan to **HEAR** this scale, or go directly to flametreemusic.com

128

F Natural Minor

START
HERE

ALL THE
BASICS

NOTES &
TIMING

PITCH

KEYS
SIGNATURE

SCALES

COMMON
CHORDS

EXTRA
NOTATION

Scale notes	Up	F G A♭ B♭ C D♭ E♭ F
	Down	F E♭ D♭ C B♭ A♭ G F

FREE ACCESS on iPhone & Android etc, using any free QR code app

Scan to **HEAR** this scale, or go directly to flametreemusic.com

START
HERE

ALL THE
BASICS

NOTES &
TIMING

PITCH

KEYS

SCALES

COMMON
CHORDS

EXTRA
NOTATION

F Harmonic Minor

Scale notes	Up	F G A♭ B♭ C D♭ E F
	Down	F E D♭ C B♭ A♭ G F

FREE ACCESS on iPhone & Android
etc, using any free QR code app

Scan to **HEAR** this scale, or go directly
to flametreemusic.com

F Melodic Minor

Scale notes	Up	F G A♭ B♭ C D E F
	Down	F E♭ D♭ C B♭ A♭ G F

FREE ACCESS on iPhone & Android etc, using any free QR code app

Scan to **HEAR** this scale, or go directly to flametreemusic.com

SCALES

F♯ Major

START
HERE

ALL THE
BASICS

NOTES &
TIMING

PITCH

KEYS

SCALES

COMMON
CHORDS

EXTRA
NOTATION

Scale notes	Up	F♯ G♯ A♯ B C♯ D♯ E♯ F♯
	Down	F♯ E♯ D♯ C♯ B A♯ G♯ F♯

FREE ACCESS on iPhone & Android
etc, using any free QR code app

Scan to **HEAR** this scale, or go directly
to flametreemusic.com

F♯ Natural Minor

START
HERE

ALL THE
BASICS

NOTES &
TIMING

PITCH

KEYS
SIGNATURE

SCALES

COMMON
CHORDS

EXTRA
NOTATION

Scale notes	Up	F♯ G♯ A B C♯ D E F♯
	Down	F♯ E D C♯ B A G♯ F♯

FREE ACCESS on iPhone & Android
etc, using any free QR code app

Scan to **HEAR** this scale, or go directly
to flametreemusic.com

F♯ Harmonic Minor

Scale notes	Up	F♯ G♯ A B C♯ D E♯ F♯
	Down	F♯ E♯ D C♯ B A G♯ F♯

FREE ACCESS on iPhone & Android etc, using any free QR code app

Scan to **HEAR** this scale, or go directly to flametreemusic.com

START HERE

ALL THE BASICS

NOTES & TIMING

PITCH

KEYS

SCALES

COMMON CHORDS

EXTRA NOTATION

F# Melodic Minor

START
HERE

ALL THE
BASICS

NOTES &
TIMING

PITCH

KEYS
SIGNATURE

SCALES

COMMON
CHORDS

EXTRA

Scale notes		
	Up	F# G# A B C# D# E# F#
	Down	F# E♮ D♮ C# B A G# F#

G Major

ALL THE BASICS

NOTES & TIMING

PITCH

KEYS

SCALES

COMMON CHORDS

EXTRA NOTATION

Scale notes	Up	G A B C D E F♯ G
	Down	G F♯ E D C B A G

FREE ACCESS on iPhone & Android etc, using any free QR code app

Scan to **HEAR** this scale, or go directly to flametreemusic.com

136

G Natural Minor

Scale notes	Up	G A B♭ C D E♭ F G
	Down	G F E♭ D C B♭ A G

Scan to **HEAR** this scale, or go directly to flametreemusic.com

SCALES

G Harmonic Minor

Scale notes	Up	G A B♭ C D E♭ F♯ G
	Down	G F♯ E♭ D C B♭ A G

Scan to **HEAR** this scale, or go directly to flametreemusic.com

START HERE

ALL THE BASICS

NOTES & TIMING

PITCH

KEYS

SCALES

COMMON CHORDS

EXTRA NOTATION

G Melodic Minor

START HERE

ALL THE BASICS

NOTES & TIMING

PITCH

KEYS SIGNATURE

SCALES

COMMON CHORDS

EXTRA NOTATION

Scale notes	Up	G A B♭ C D E F♯ G
	Down	G F♮ E♭ D C B♭ A G

FREE ACCESS on iPhone & Android etc, using any free QR code app

Scan to **HEAR** this scale, or go directly to flametreemusic.com

139

A♭ Major

Scale notes	Up	A♭ B♭ C D♭ E♭ F G A♭
	Down	A♭ G F E♭ D♭ C B♭ A♭

Scan to **HEAR** this scale, or go directly to flametreemusic.com

G♯ Natural Minor

START HERE

ALL THE BASICS

NOTES & TIMING

PITCH

KEYS SIGNATURE

SCALES

COMMON CHORDS

EXTRA NOTATION

Scale notes	Up	G♯ A♯ B C♯ D♯ E F♯ G♯
	Down	G♯ F♯ E D♯ C♯ B A♯ G♯

FREE ACCESS on iPhone & Android etc, using any free QR code app

Scan to **HEAR** this scale, or go directly to flametreemusic.com

G♯ Harmonic Minor

This double sharp symbol raises the note by two semitones.

	Up	G♯ A♯ B C♯ D♯ E F𝄪 G♯
Scale notes	Down	G♯ F𝄪 E D♯ C♯ B A♯ G♯

Scan to **HEAR** this scale, or go directly to flametreemusic.com

G♯ Melodic Minor

Scale notes	Up	G♯ A♯ B C♯ D♯ E♯ F× G♯
	Down	G♯ F× E♮ D♯ C♯ B A♯ G♯

FREE ACCESS on iPhone & Android etc, using any free QR code app

Scan to **HEAR** this scale, or go directly to flametreemusic.com

START HERE

ALL THE BASICS

NOTES & TIMING

PITCH

KEYS SIGNATURE

SCALES

COMMON CHORDS

EXTRA NOTATION

A Major

START
HERE

ALL THE
BASICS

NOTES &
TIMING

PITCH

KEYS

SCALES

COMMON
CHORDS

EXTRA
NOTATION

Scale notes	Up	A B C♯ D E F♯ G♯ A
	Down	A G♯ F♯ E D C♯ B A

FREE ACCESS on iPhone & Android
etc, using any free QR code app

Scan to **HEAR** this scale, or go directly
to flametreemusic.com

A Natural Minor

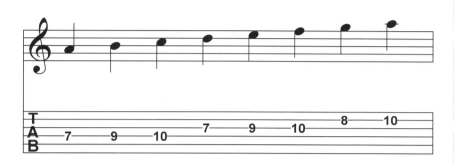

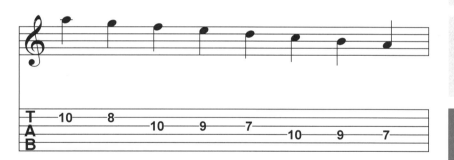

Scale notes	Up	A B C D E F G A
	Down	A G F E D C B A

FREE ACCESS on iPhone & Android
etc, using any free QR code app

Scan to **HEAR** this scale, or go directly
to flametreemusic.com

START
HERE

ALL THE
BASICS

NOTES &
TIMING

PITCH

KEYS

SCALES

COMMON
CHORDS

EXTRA
NOTATION

A Harmonic Minor

Scale notes	Up	A B C D E F G♯ A
	Down	A G♯ F E D C B A

Scan to **HEAR** this scale, or go directly to flametreemusic.com

A Melodic Minor

START
HERE

ALL THE
BASICS

NOTES &
TIMING

PITCH

KEYS
SIGNATURE

SCALES

COMMON
CHORDS

EXTRA
NOTATION

Scale notes	Up	A B C D E F♯ G♯ A
	Down	A G♮ F♮ E D C B A

FREE ACCESS on iPhone & Android etc, using any free QR code app

Scan to **HEAR** this scale, or go directly to flametreemusic.com

147

B♭ Major

START
HERE

ALL THE
BASICS

NOTES &
TIMING

PITCH

KEYS

SCALES

COMMON
CHORDS

EXTRA
NOTATION

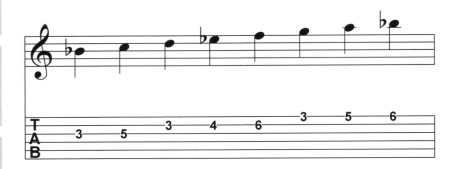

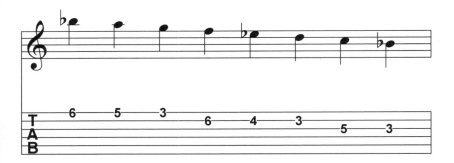

Scale notes	Up	B♭ C D E♭ F G A B♭
	Down	B♭ A G F E♭ D C B♭

FREE ACCESS on iPhone & Android
etc, using any free QR code app

Scan to **HEAR** this scale, or go directly
to flametreemusic.com

B♭ Natural Minor

START HERE

ALL THE BASICS

NOTES & TIMING

PITCH

KEYS SIGNATURE

SCALES

COMMON CHORDS

EXTRA NOTATION

Scale notes

Up   B♭ C D♭ E♭ F G♭ A♭ B♭
Down   B♭ A♭ G♭ F E♭ D♭ C B♭

FREE ACCESS on iPhone & Android etc, using any free QR code app

Scan to **HEAR** this scale, or go directly to flametreemusic.com

B♭ Harmonic Minor

START
HERE

ALL THE
BASICS

NOTES &
TIMING

PITCH

KEYS

SCALES

COMMON
CHORDS

EXTRA
NOTATION

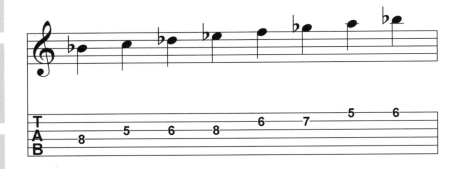

Scale notes	Up	B♭ C D♭ E♭ F G♭ A B♭
	Down	B♭ A G♭ F E♭ D♭ C B♭

FREE ACCESS on iPhone & Android
etc, using any free QR code app

Scan to **HEAR** this scale, or go directly
to flametreemusic.com

B♭ Melodic Minor

Scale notes	Up	B♭ C D♭ E♭ F G A B♭
	Down	B♭ A♭ G♭ F E♭ D♭ C B♭

FREE ACCESS on iPhone & Android etc, using any free QR code app

Scan to **HEAR** this scale, or go directly to flametreemusic.com

151

START HERE

ALL THE BASICS

NOTES & TIMING

PITCH

KEYS SIGNATURE

SCALES

COMMON CHORDS

EXTRA NOTATION

B Major

Scale notes	Up	B C♯ D♯ E F♯ G♯ A♯ B
	Down	B A♯ G♯ F♯ E D♯ C♯ B

FREE ACCESS on iPhone & Android etc, using any free QR code app

Scan to **HEAR** this scale, or go directly to flametreemusic.com

START HERE

ALL THE BASICS

NOTES & TIMING

PITCH

KEYS

SCALES

COMMON CHORDS

EXTRA NOTATION

B Natural Minor

Scale notes	Up	B C# D E F# G A B
	Down	B A G F# E D C# B

START HERE

ALL THE BASICS

NOTES & TIMING

PITCH

KEYS SIGNATURE

SCALES

COMMON CHORDS

EXTRA NOTATION

FREE ACCESS on iPhone & Android etc, using any free QR code app

Scan to **HEAR** this scale, or go directly to flametreemusic.com

153

B Harmonic Minor

START
HERE

ALL THE
BASICS

NOTES &
TIMING

PITCH

KEYS

SCALES

COMMON
CHORDS

EXTRA
NOTATION

Scale notes	Up	B C♯ D E F♯ G A♯ B
	Down	B A♯ G F♯ E D C♯ B

FREE ACCESS on iPhone & Android
etc, using any free QR code app

Scan to **HEAR** this scale, or go directly
to flametreemusic.com

B Melodic Minor

START
HERE

ALL THE
BASICS

NOTES &
TIMING

PITCH

KEYS
SIGNATURE

SCALES

COMMON
CHORDS

EXTRA
NOTATION

Scale notes	Up	B C♯ D E F♯ G♯ A♯ B
	Down	B A♮ G♮ F♯ E D C♯ B

FREE ACCESS on iPhone & Android
etc, using any free QR code app

Scan to **HEAR** this scale, or go directly
to flametreemusic.com

Chords

We've looked at single notes played one at a time, so now it's time to move on to chords, which can be used to accompany single-line melodies. Chords add richness and depth to music and can be played on any instrument capable of making more than one sound at a time: such as a keyboard, guitar, or harp.

Chords from Scales

For rock, blues and folk musicians, chords often provide the backbone to their songwriting. Melodic instruments and voices joined together also create a chord-like sound, with many melodies joining in a series of chord-like structures.

If you know which **key** to start in, you can identify which chords will work in that key.

Simple chords are called **triads** because they are made up of **three notes**.

To find the simple triad chords from a scale, use **any note** within to **start**, then **add** the **note two up**, then **add** the note two up again.

The **root** note of a chord is the **lowest** note: for example, the C major chord will have C as its root, and D major will have D as its root.

Each QR code at the bottom of the pages in this section will bring you to each key's relevant root chord on flametreemusic.com.

FREE ACCESS on iPhone & Android
etc, using any free QR code app

Scan to **HEAR** the C major chord, and access the full library of scales and chords on flametreemusic.com

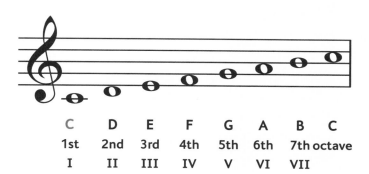

C	D	E	F	G	A	B	C
1st	2nd	3rd	4th	5th	6th	7th	octave
I	II	III	IV	V	VI	VII	

START HERE

ALL THE BASICS

NOTES & TIMING

PITCH

KEYS

SCALES

COMMON CHORDS

EXTRA NOTATION

C Major chord

1st + 3rd + 5th notes of the C Major scale

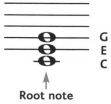

G
E
C

Root note

F Major chord

4th + 6th + octave notes of the C Major scale

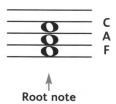

C
A
F

Root note

G Major chord

5th + 7th + high 2nd notes of the C Major scale

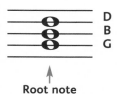

D
B
G

Root note

FREE ACCESS on iPhone & Android etc, using any free QR code app

Scan to **HEAR** the C major chord, and access the full library of scales and chords on flametreemusic.com

Chord Inversions

A chord that has a bottom note other than its root note is called an inverted chord.

Inverted chords are used to add colour and **variety** to a musical piece. A bass or double bass might play the root notes while the keyboard or string players might play an inverted chord above the root note.

As an example, the C major chord can be played with the **root note** of **C**, or the **E** or the **G**.

The following pages give some of the most common chords that are formed from the major scales.

Scan to **HEAR** the C major chord, and access the full library of scales and chords on flametreemusic.com

START HERE

ALL THE BASICS

NOTES & TIMING

PITCH

KEYS

SCALES

COMMON CHORDS

EXTRA NOTATION

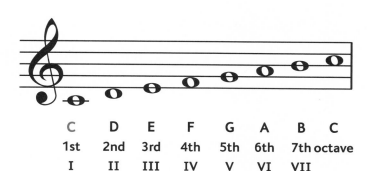

C	D	E	F	G	A	B	C
1st	2nd	3rd	4th	5th	6th	7th	octave
I	II	III	IV	V	VI	VII	

C Major chord

1st, 3rd and 5th notes of the C Major scale

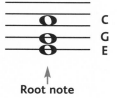

G
E
C

↑
Root note

C Major 1st Inversion

3rd and 5th and octave notes of the C Major scale

C
G
E

↑
Root note

C Major 2nd Inversion

5th, octave and high 3rd notes of the C Major scale

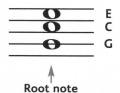

E
C
G

↑
Root note

START HERE

ALL THE BASICS

NOTES & TIMING

PITCH

KEYS

SCALES

COMMON CHORDS

EXTRA NOTATION

Common Chords of the
C Major Scale

START
HERE

ALL THE
BASICS

NOTES &
TIMING

PITCH

KEYS

SCALES

COMMON
CHORDS

EXTRA
NOTATION

Notes

C	D	E	F	G	A	B
I	II	III	IV	V	VI	VII

Chord IV
IV, VI, I
F Major
Notes: F, A, C

Chord I
I, III, V
C Major
Notes: C, E, G

Chord V
V, VII, II
G Major
Notes: G, B, D

Chord II
II, IV, VI
D Minor
Notes: D, F, A

Chord VI
VI, I, III
A Minor
Notes: A, C, E

FREE ACCESS on iPhone & Android
etc, using any free QR code app

Scan to **HEAR** this key's chords, or go
directly to flametreemusic.com

Common Chords of the
D♭ Major Scale

Notes

D♭	E♭	F♭	G♭	A♭	B♭	C♭
I	II	III	IV	V	VI	VII

Chord IV
IV, VI, I
G♭ Major
Notes: G♭, B♭, D♭

Chord I
I, III, V
D♭ Major
Notes: D♭, F, A♭

Chord V
V, VII, II
A♭ Major
Notes: A♭, C, E♭

Chord II
II, IV, VI
E♭ Minor
Notes: E♭, G♭, B♭

Chord VI
VI, I, III
B♭ Minor
Notes: B♭, D♭, F

START HERE

ALL THE BASICS

NOTES & TIMING

PITCH

KEYS

SCALES

COMMON CHORDS

EXTRA NOTATION

FREE ACCESS on iPhone & Android etc, using any free QR code app

Scan to **HEAR** this key's chords, or go directly to flametreemusic.com

Common Chords of the
D Major Scale

START
HERE

ALL THE
BASICS

NOTES &
TIMING

PITCH

KEYS

SCALES

COMMON
CHORDS

EXTRA
NOTATION

Notes

D	E	F#	G	A	B	C#
I	II	III	IV	V	VI	VII

Chord IV
IV, VI, I
G Major
Notes: G, B, D

Chord I
I, III, V
D Major
Notes: D, F# A

Chord V
V, VII, II
A Major
Notes: A, C# E

Chord II
II, IV, VI
E Minor
Notes: E, G, B

Chord VI
VI, I, III
B Minor
Notes: B, D# F#

FREE ACCESS on iPhone & Android
etc, using any free QR code app

Scan to **HEAR** this key's chords, or go
directly to flametreemusic.com

Common Chords of the
E♭ Major Scale

Notes

E♭	F	G	A♭	B♭	C	D
I	II	III	IV	V	VI	VII

Chord IV
IV, VI, I
A♭ Major
Notes: A♭, C, E♭

Chord I
I, III, V
E♭ Major
Notes: E♭, G, B♭

Chord V
V, VII, II
B♭ Major
Notes: B♭, D, F

Chord II
II, IV, VI
F Minor
Notes: F, A♭, C

Chord VI
VI, I, III
C Minor
Notes: C, E♭, G

START HERE

ALL THE BASICS

NOTES & TIMING

PITCH

KEYS

SCALES

COMMON CHORDS

EXTRA NOTATION

FREE ACCESS on iPhone & Android etc, using any free QR code app

Scan to **HEAR** this key's chords, or go directly to flametreemusic.com

Common Chords of the
E Major Scale

START
HERE

ALL THE
BASICS

NOTES &
TIMING

PITCH

KEYS

SCALES

COMMON
CHORDS

EXTRA
NOTATION

Notes

E	F♯	G♯	A	B	C♯	D♯
I	II	III	IV	V	VI	VII

Chord IV
IV, VI, I
A Major
Notes: A, C♯ E

Chord I
I, III, V
E Major
Notes: E, G♯ B

Chord V
V, VII, II
B Major
Notes: B, D♯ F♯

Chord II
II, IV, VI
F♯ Minor
Notes: F♯ A, C♯

Chord VI
VI, I, III
C♯ Minor
Notes: C♯ E, G♯

FREE ACCESS on iPhone & Android
etc, using any free QR code app

Scan to **HEAR** this key's chords, or go
directly to flametreemusic.com

Common Chords of the
F Major Scale

START HERE

ALL THE BASICS

NOTES & TIMING

PITCH

KEYS

SCALES

COMMON CHORDS

EXTRA NOTATION

Notes

F	G	A	B♭	C	D	E
I	II	III	IV	V	VI	VII

Chord IV
IV, VI, I
B♭ Major
Notes: B♭, D, F

Chord I
I, III, V
F Major
Notes: F, A, C

Chord V
V, VII, II
C Major
Notes: C, E, G

Chord II
II, IV, VI
G Minor
Notes: G, B♭, D

Chord VI
VI, I, III
D Minor
Notes: D, F, A

FREE ACCESS on iPhone & Android etc, using any free QR code app

Scan to **HEAR** this key's chords, or go directly to flametreemusic.com

Common Chords of the
F# Major Scale

START
HERE

ALL THE
BASICS

NOTES &
TIMING

PITCH

KEYS

SCALES

COMMON
CHORDS

EXTRA
NOTATION

Notes

F#	G#	A#	B	C#	D#	E#
I	II	III	IV	V	VI	VII

Chord IV
IV, VI, I
B Major
Notes: B, D#, F#

Chord I
I, III, V
F# Major
Notes: F#, A#, C#

Chord V
V, VII, II
C# Major
Notes: C#, E#, G#

Chord II
II, IV, VI
G# Minor
Notes: G#, B, D#

Chord VI
VI, I, III
D# Minor
Notes: D#, F#, A#

FREE ACCESS on iPhone & Android
etc, using any free QR code app

Scan to **HEAR** this key's chords, or go
directly to flametreemusic.com

Common Chords of the
G Major Scale

Notes

G A B C D E F♯

I II III IV V VI VII

Chord I
I, III, V
G Major
Notes: G, B, D

Chord II
II, IV, VI
A Minor
Notes: A, C, E

Chord IV
IV, VI, I
C Major
Notes: C, E, G

Chord V
V, VII, II
D Major
Notes: D, F♯ A

Chord VI
VI, I, III
E Minor
Notes: E, G, B

FREE ACCESS on iPhone & Android etc, using any free QR code app

Scan to **HEAR** this key's chords, or go directly to flametreemusic.com

START HERE

ALL THE BASICS

NOTES & TIMING

PITCH

KEYS

SCALES

COMMON CHORDS

EXTRA NOTATION

START
HERE

ALL THE
BASICS

NOTES &
TIMING

PITCH

KEYS

SCALES

COMMON
CHORDS

EXTRA
NOTATION

Common Chords of the

A♭ Major Scale

Notes

A♭	B♭	C	D♭	E♭	F	G
I	II	III	IV	V	VI	VII

Chord IV
IV, VI, I
D♭ Major
Notes: D♭, F, A♭

Chord I
I, III, V
A♭ Major
Notes: A♭, C, E♭

Chord V
V, VII, II
E♭ Major
Notes: E♭, G, B♭

Chord II
II, IV, VI
B♭ Minor
Notes: B♭, D♭, F

Chord VI
VI, I, III
F Minor
Notes: F, A♭, C

FREE ACCESS on iPhone & Android
etc, using any free QR code app

Scan to **HEAR** this key's chords, or go
directly to flametreemusic.com

Common Chords of the

A Major Scale

START
HERE

ALL THE
BASICS

NOTES &
TIMING

PITCH

KEYS

SCALES

COMMON
CHORDS

EXTRA
NOTATION

Notes

A   B   C♯   D   E   F♯   G♯

I   II   III   IV   V   VI   VII

Chord IV
IV, VI, I
D Major
Notes: D, F♯ A

Chord I
I, III, V
A Major
Notes: A, C♯ E

Chord V
V, VII, II
E Major
Notes: E, G♯ B

Chord II
II, IV, VI
B Minor
Notes: B, D, F♯

Chord VI
VI, I, III
F♯ Minor
Notes: F♯ A, C♯

Scan to **HEAR** this key's chords, or go
directly to flametreemusic.com

Common Chords of the
B♭ Major Scale

START
HERE

ALL THE
BASICS

NOTES &
TIMING

PITCH

KEYS

SCALES

COMMON
CHORDS

EXTRA
NOTATION

Notes

B♭	C	D	E♭	F	G	A
I	II	III	IV	V	VI	VII

Chord IV
IV, VI, I
E♭ Major
Notes: E♭, G, B♭

Chord I
I, III, V
B♭ Major
Notes: B♭, D, F

Chord V
V, VII, II
F Major
Notes: F, A, C

Chord II
II, IV, VI
C Minor
Notes: C, E♭, G

Chord VI
VI, I, III
G Minor
Notes: G, B♭, D

FREE ACCESS on iPhone & Android
etc, using any free QR code app

Scan to **HEAR** this key's chords, or go
directly to flametreemusic.com

Common Chords of the
B Major Scale

Notes

B	C♯	D♯	E	F♯	G♯	A♯
I	II	III	IV	V	VI	VII

Chord IV
IV, VI, I
E Major
Notes: E, G♯ B

Chord I
I, III, V
B Major
Notes: B, D♯ F♯

Chord V
V, VII, II
F♯ Major
Notes: F♯ A♯ C♯

Chord II
II, IV, VI
C♯ Minor
Notes: C♯ E, G♯

Chord VI
VI, I, III
G♯ Minor
Notes: G♯ B, D♯

COMMON
CHORDS

Scan to **HEAR** this key's chords, or go directly to flametreemusic.com

Expressional Marks

A musical piece is often full of symbols, all of which provide clues about how the music should be played: how loud, what speed and when to repeat.

Classical music uses a great many Italian terms because in the early 1600s Italy was the cultural centre of European music. Church choral music moved to broader orchestral forms, the major and minor scales were standardized and tonal music gained great influence, resulting in the western classical style. The twentieth century brought an explosion of new styles of music (blues, jazz, rock) and with them the greater use of English terms.

Scan to **HEAR** the C major chord, and access the full library of scales and chords on flametreemusic.com

START HERE

ALL THE BASICS

NOTES & TIMING

PITCH

KEYS

SCALES

COMMON CHORDS

EXTRA
NOTATION

Tempo

These marks are written above the music and show how quickly to play the music.

lento or *adagio*	slowly
andante	at walking speed
moderato	moderate speed
allegretto	fairly fast
allegro	fast
presto	very fast
ritardando (rit.)	slowing down
accelerando (accel.)	getting faster
a tempo	at original speed
piu mosso	faster
meno mosso	slower
ad lib./ad libitum	freely

Dynamics

These marks are written below the notes and show how loudly to play the music.

pp	*pianissimo*	very quiet
p	*piano*	quiet
mp	*mezzopiano*	fairly quiet
mf	*mezzoforte*	fairly loud
f	*forte*	loud
ff	*fortissimo*	very loud
◁	*crescendo (cresc.)*	growing louder
▷	*diminuendo (dim.)*	growing quieter

START HERE

ALL THE BASICS

NOTES & TIMING

PITCH

KEYS

SCALES

COMMON CHORDS

EXTRA NOTATION

FREE ACCESS on iPhone & Android etc, using any free QR code app

Scan to **HEAR** the C major chord, and access the full library of scales and chords on flametreemusic.com

START
HERE

ALL THE
BASICS

NOTES &
TIMING

PITCH

KEYS

SCALES

COMMON
CHORDS

EXTRA
NOTATION

Articulation

These marks are written above or below the notes and show how to play the notes.

.	*staccato*	short
>	*accento*	accented
∧	*marcato*	louder accent
—	*tenuto*	slightly stressed
⌒	*legato*	slur, smooth
sfz	*sforzando*	forced, heavy accent
fp	*fortepiano*	loud attack then quiet
⌢	*fermata*	hold, pause
8ᵛᵃ	*all' ottava*	one octave higher than written
8ᵃᵇ	*ottava bassa*	one octave lower than written
tr ∿∿∿∿∿		trill

Other Symbols

D.C. al Fine	Return to the beginning and play to ***Fine*** (end).
D.S. al Fine	Return to 𝄋 and play to ***Fine***.
D.C. al Coda	Return to the beginning, play to ⊕ and skip to Coda.
D.S. al Coda	Return to 𝄋 , play to ⊕ and skip to Coda.

𝄇   Return to the beginning or nearest repeat sign.   𝄆

FREE ACCESS on iPhone & Android
etc, using any free QR code app

Scan to **HEAR** the C major chord, and access the full library of scales and chords on flametreemusic.com

START
HERE

ALL THE
BASICS

NOTES &
TIMING

PITCH

KEYS

SCALES

COMMON
CHORDS

EXTRA
NOTATION

FREE ACCESS on iPhone & Android
etc, using any free QR code app

Scan to **HEAR** the C major chord, and
access the full library of scales and
chords on flametreemusic.com

flametreemusic.com

The Flame Tree Music website complements our range of print books and offers easy access to chords and scales online, and on the move, through tablets, smartphones, and desktop computers.

1. The site offers access to chord diagrams and finger positions for both the guitar and the piano/keyboard, presenting a wide range of sound options to help develop good listening technique, and to assist you in identifying the chord and each note within it.

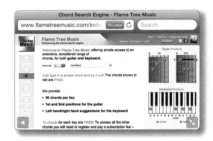

2. The site offers 12 **free** chords, those most commonly used in bands and songwriting.

3. A subscription is available if you'd like the full range of chords, **50** for **each key**.

4. Guitar chords are shown with **first** and **second positions on the fretboard**.

5. For the keyboard, you can **see** and **hear** each note in **left-** and **right-hand positions**.

6. Choose the key, then the chord name from the drop down menu. Note that the **red chords** are available **free**. Those in blue can be accessed with a subscription.

7. Once you've selected the chord, press **GO** and the details of the chord will be shown, with chord spellings, keyboard and guitar fingerings.

8. Sounds are provided in four easy-to-understand configurations.

9. flametreemusic.com also gives you access to **20 scales for each key**.